Contents

4 dört

GET BY IN
TURKISH

A quick beginners' course in spoken Turkish for holidaymakers and businesspeople

Course writer
Bengisu Rona
Lecturer in Turkish Studies
School of Oriental and
African Studies
University of London

Producer
Alan Wilding

BBC Books

Get by in Turkish
A BBC Radio course
First broadcast in Spring 1989

Published to accompany a series
of programmes prepared in
consultation with the BBC
Educational Broadcasting Council

Illustrations by Sue Henry
Cover designed by Peter Bridgewater
and Annie Moss

Published by BBC Books, an imprint of BBC Worldwide Publishing.
BBC Worldwide Ltd., Woodlands, 80 Wood Lane,
London W12 0TT.

ISBN 0 563 39985 6
First published in 1989
This edition published in 1995
Reprinted 1995, 1996
© The author and the British Broadcasting Corporation 1989

Printed and bound in Great Britain by Clays Ltd, St Ives plc
Cover printed by Clays Ltd, St Ives plc

About Turkish

Turkish is spoken by 55 million people in Turkey (the population increases by about a million a year), and by some one million Turks in Bulgaria, as well as by Turkish communities in Yugoslavia, Cyprus and northern Greece.

There are also Turks living in western Europe: over a million in West Germany and West Berlin. And there is a sizeable community in London. Turkish is not related either to other European languages or to Arabic (although, until 1928, it was written in the Arabic script, and you will still see inscriptions on monuments in Arabic lettering). Almost all Turks are Moslems, and Turkish has acquired a large number of words from Arabic, the language of Islam, and Persian.

It is a distinct advantage to foreigners that words are pronounced exactly as they are spelt (there's a guide to pronunciation on page 7) – unlike English, where foreigners (and even native speakers) have difficulty in learning how to spell.

By European standards, Turkish grammar is very straightforward: when you have learnt how to use one verb, for example, you have learnt how to use all of them. There are hardly any exceptions. And there are a number of words borrowed from English and French: *taksi* ('taxi'), *kaset* ('cassette'), *garson* ('waiter') and *mersi* ('thank you').

Not many foreigners take the trouble to try and speak Turkish, although Turkey has recently become very popular as a holiday destination. And any foreigner who does make the effort to learn some of the language will usually be greeted with considerable enthusiasm, respect and hospitality.

About 'Get by in Turkish'

Get by in Turkish is an introduction to the basic language you'll find useful on a trip to Turkey. It consists of:

● this book

● a pack of two cassettes

● six BBC Radio programmes

Naturally the radio programmes will not always be on the air; the book and cassettes are designed to give you a concentrated form of the programmes so that you can learn in your own time and at your own speed.

The programmes contain:

● real-life conversations recorded mostly in Istanbul, in which Turkish people go to cafés and restaurants, do their shopping, visit places of interest, travel around and meet each other

● plenty of opportunities for you to acquire and practise the basics

The book contains:

● advice on how to pronounce the language

● the texts of the conversations in the programmes and on the cassettes (numbers in the conversations refer to the language explanations in each chapter)

● key phrases to help you understand the conversations

● explanations of how the language works

● useful tips for a trip to Turkey

● exercises (with answers) so that you can check your progress after each chapter; a full 'test' at the end, called 'Can you get by?', so that you can test and mark yourself

● a reference section with word lists, answers to the exercises, and a basic grammar section

The cassettes contain:

- a pronunciation guide so that you can learn the sounds of Turkish and learn to pronounce correctly any word you read
- the conversations from the book and programmes, with extra conversations not in the programmes
- explanations of how the language works
- extra opportunities to practise aloud

Some tips on learning a language

Basically, it is all a question of time. The amount of time needed varies from person to person, but if something is not clear to you, come back to it later.

Try to learn the word lists (or part of them) in each chapter *before* tackling the conversations. When you think you've memorised the word lists (or part of them), cover the English with a card and test yourself; then cover the Turkish with a card and test yourself again.

Speak aloud whenever you have the chance to, whether reading in the book or listening to the programmes and cassettes.

Do the exercises at the end of each chapter once you feel you've grasped the contents. Keep a record of your score and come back to the same exercises later to see if you can improve.

Making mistakes is normal. If you do, look back at the language notes and try to work out where you went wrong.

Good luck!

How to pronounce Turkish

The Turkish alphabet has 29 letters: 8 vowels and 21 consonants. Quite a number of them are similar to their English equivalents.

The vowels

a like the 'u' in the English word 'b*u*s' (*at* horse)

e as in 'g*e*m' or 'p*e*n' (*ev* house)

i as in 'b*i*t', 'r*i*sk' (*bir* one)

ı like the English article 'a' in 'a book', or the final 'a' in Malta or Burma

o like the first vowel in the world '*o*live' (*oda* room)

ö like the vowel sound in 'd*i*rt' but short (*dört* four)

u as in 'p*u*t' (*su* water)

ü as in the name of the German city D*ü*sseldorf (*üç* three)

You will occasionally see an accent (ˆ) on vowels. It is found on some borrowed words (*bekâr* unmarried).

The consonants

The sounds represented by b, d, f, h, k, l, m, n, p, s, t, v, y and z are similar to their English counterparts in almost all contexts. Otherwise:

c as in '*j*am', '*J*ohn', '*g*in' (*cin* gin)

ç is *ch* in English, as in '*ch*urch', '*ch*ild' (*üç* three)

g as in '*g*o', '*g*ale' (*git* go)

ğ this letter has no distinct pronunciation. It serves to lengthen the vowel that comes before it, e.g. *dağ* (mountain) is uttered as a 'd' followed by a long 'a'

j as in 'plea*s*ure', 'rou*g*e' (*plaj* beach)

r is rolled between two vowels (*bira* beer) and it is pronounced fully when at the end of a word (*bir* one; *var* there is/are)

ş is *sh* in English, as in *sh*oe (*şiş* skewer)

The letters q, w and x do not exist in the Turkish alphabet. Where these letters occur in foreign words which are commonly used in Turkish, like *taksi* ('taxi') and *ekspres* ('express'), the 'x' sound is written as *ks*. A 'w' is often written and pronounced as *v* in Turkish – e.g. 'whisky' is *viski*.

Vowel harmony

Turkish uses endings to build up words and grammatical features. For example, 'I am at home' consists of four words in English, but this is reduced to just one word in Turkish: *evdeyim*. The word *evdeyim* is made up of three separate parts: the basic word *ev* meaning 'house' or 'home', plus two endings – *-de* ('at'), and *-yim* ('I am'). 'At' and 'I am' come after the word *ev* ('home') in Turkish, not before as in English.

This building-up of words using different endings is governed by an interesting feature of Turkish: **vowel harmony**. The vowels used in the various endings differ depending on the last vowel in the basic word.

Four of the eight vowels in Turkish are 'front' vowels (e, i, ö, ü) and four are 'back' (a, ı, o, u). If the last vowel of the basic word is a front vowel, then the vowel in the ending will also be a front vowel. If the last vowel is a back vowel, then the ending will also have a back vowel. For example:

ev house   *evler* houses   *evlerde* in the houses

oda room   *odalar* rooms   *odalarda* in the rooms

Some suffixes have more possibilities. One of the most common – and useful – is to form abstract nouns. Thus:

uzun means 'long'   *uzunluk* means 'length'
sıcak means 'hot'   *sıcaklık* means 'heat'
iyi means 'good'   *iyilik* means 'goodness'
güç means 'difficult'   *güçlük* means 'difficulty'

Other suffixes are used where we would use prepositions (words like 'to', 'with', 'from') in English:

şeker sugar	*şeker**li*** with sugar
yumurta egg	*yumurta**lı*** with egg
süt milk	*süt**lü*** with milk
tuz salt	*tuz**lu*** with salt

The full rules of vowel harmony sound rather complicated, but you will find that it quickly becomes instinctive, and because there are few exceptions to the grammatical rules in Turkish, it makes the language easier, rather than more difficult, to learn.

1 Ordering your drinks

Key words and phrases

Counting

bir, iki, üç	one, two, three

To order a drink

Bir çay lütfen.	A tea, please.
İki çay lütfen.	Two teas, please.

To ask 'have you got . . .?'

(Bira) var mı?	Is there any (beer)?

To ask for the bill

Hesap lütfen.	The bill, please.

To say thank you/thanks

Teşekkür ederim/Teşekkürler.

Conversations

1 Two teas, please.

The following conversations were all recorded in Turkish cafés and tea-houses.

WOMAN	Garson, lütfen.
WAITER	Buyurun[1] efendim[2].
WOMAN	İki çay lütfen.
WAITER	Peki efendim.

2 Is there any beer?

WAITER	Buyurun. Ne içersiniz[3]?
WOMAN	Bira var mı[3]?
WAITER	Var.
WOMAN	İki bira lütfen.
WAITER	Tabii.

3 There is no beer, so two Turkish coffees.

WOMAN	Garson, bir bira, bir kahve.
WAITER	Bira yok.
WOMAN	İki kahve.

WAITER Türk kahvesi mi, neskafe mi[4] efendim?
WOMAN Türk kahvesi[5], sade.
WAITER Peki efendim.

4 Three coffees: one medium-sweet, one without sugar, one sweet.

WOMAN Garson, lütfen.
WAITER Buyurun.
WOMAN Üç kahve[6]; bir orta, bir sade, bir şekerli.
WAITER Tabii efendim.

5 One beer, one coffee . . .

WAITER Buyurun.
WOMAN Bir bira, bir kahve lütfen.
WAITER Bira yok.
WOMAN İki kahve.
WAITER Nasıl?
WOMAN İki orta lütfen.
WAITER Peki.

6 . . . and the bill, please.

WOMAN Garson.
WAITER Buyurun efendim.
WOMAN Hesap[7] lütfen.
WAITER Altı yüz lira efendim.
WOMAN Buyurun.
WAITER Teşekkürler efendim.

7 An instant coffee, with milk.

WAITER Buyurun efendim.
WOMAN Bir neskafe lütfen.
WAITER Sütlü[8] mü, sütsüz mü?
WOMAN Sütlü.
WAITER Peki efendim.

8 A tea, a coffee and a fruit juice . . .

WAITER Buyurun efendim.
WOMAN Bir çay, bir kahve, bir meyve suyu lütfen.
WAITER Meyve suyu neli?
WOMAN Portakal.
WAITER Kahve nasıl?
WOMAN Sade lütfen.
WAITER Peki efendim.

9 . . . and asking for the bill.

WOMAN Hesap lütfen.
WAITER Tabii efendim. Bin yüz lira.
WOMAN Tamam, buyurun, üstü kalsın.
WAITER Teşekkür ederim.

10 If they don't sell alcoholic drinks . . .

WAITER Buyurun.
WOMAN İki rakı lütfen.
WAITER Rakı yok.

11 . . . ask them what they have.

WOMAN Ne var?
WAITER Çay, kahve, kola, fanta, elma.
WOMAN İki çay lütfen.
WAITER Peki.

12 Asking for a large bottle of water.

WAITER Buyurun.
WOMAN Bir büyük[9] şişe su lütfen.
WAITER Büyük yok.
WOMAN Küçük var mı?
WAITER Var.
WOMAN İki küçük lütfen.
WAITER Peki.

Word list

ne içersiniz?	what would you like to drink?
bira	beer
çay	tea
elma	apple (here, apple-flavoured tea)
fanta	fizzy orange
şeker	sugar
kahve	coffee
sade	plain (no sugar)
orta	medium sweet
şekerli	sweet
şekersiz	without sugar
kola	coke
meyve suyu	fruit juice
neskafe	instant coffee
portakal	orange
rakı	strong aniseed-flavoured alcoholic drink
su	water

süt	milk
sütlü	with milk
sütsüz	without milk
şişe	bottle
Türk kahvesi	Turkish coffee
buyurun	yes? can I help you?
efendim	sir, madam
garson	waiter
hesap	the bill
lütfen	please
peki } *tamam*	OK
üstü kalsın	keep the change
var	there is/there are
yok	there isn't/there aren't
altı	six
altı yüz	six hundred
bin	thousand
bin yüz	one thousand one hundred
bir	one
iki	two
lira	lira (Turkish currency)
üç	three
yüz	hundred
hemen	at once
tabii	of course
nasıl?	how?
ne?	what?
neli?	what with? (what flavour?)
büyük	large, big
küçük	small

Explanations

1 *Buyurun*

A very common expression. It's used:
1) to ask a customer what he/she wants: 'yes?'
2) to say 'come in' when someone knocks at the door
3) to say 'here you are' when handing something over
4) to say 'go ahead' if someone asks to borrow your lighter or take an empty chair

2 *Efendim*

Efendim is the usual polite way of addressing a

14 on dört

woman or a man. If you don't catch something, you can also say *efendim?* as a question, meaning 'I beg your pardon?'

3 Questions

Listen out for questions which end in *-siniz* (or *sınız, sunuz, sünüz*) which indicates that the question is addressed to you:

Ne içersiniz?	What would you like to drink?
Çay ister misiniz?	Would you like some tea?

And you can call the waiter by saying:

Bakar mısınız?	Literally 'Would you like to look over here?'

Var (there is/there are) and *yok* (there isn't/there aren't)

To ask a question, you have to add *mi* (or *mı, mu, mü*, depending on vowel harmony – see page 9): After *var* you add *mı* for a question.

Bira var mı?	Is there any beer?
Süt var mı?	Is there any milk?

The answer will be *var* ('there is/there are') or *yok* ('There isn't/there aren't').

4 This or that?

If you ask a question with 'or' in the middle (e.g. tea or coffee), you have to put *mi* etc. twice:

Çay mı, kahve mi?	Tea or coffee?
Büyük mü, küçük mü?	Big or small?

5 In English, two nouns can come together, one being used to describe the other: onion soup, vanilla ice-cream. Turkish does the same, but the second noun has an extra ending. The extra ending can be *i, ı, u* or *ü* (or *si* etc. following a vowel) depending on vowel harmony.

çorba soup	*domates çorbası*	tomato soup
kahve coffee	*Türk kahvesi*	Turkish coffee

An exception: *su – suyu*:

su water	*meyve suyu*	fruit juice (*lit.* fruit water)

6 Plurals

To make the plural, add *-lar* or *-ler* to the end of the noun:

çay tea   *çaylar* teas
kahve coffee   *kahveler* coffees

Again, which ending you use depends on vowel harmony.

With numbers, however, the noun remains in the singular:

bir çay, iki çay   one tea, two teas
bir bira, üç bira   one beer, three beers

7 'The'

There is no word for 'the' in Turkish:
hesap the bill

8 'With' and 'without'

When talking about flavours and ingredients, 'with' and 'without' are added to the end of a noun:
'with' is *-li* (or *-lı, -lu, -lü*)
'without' is *-siz* (or *-sız, -suz, -süz*)

süt milk   *sütlü* with milk   *sütsüz* without milk
şeker sugar   *şekerli* with   *şekersiz* without
                sugar   sugar
şekerli kahve   coffee with sugar
şekersiz çay   tea without sugar
kahveli dondurma   coffee ice-cream

So the question *şekerli mi şekersiz mi?* means 'with or without sugar?' And *ne?* is 'what?', so *neli?* means 'what with?'

9 Adjectives

Adjectives come before the noun in Turkish:
*iki **büyük** şişe*   two *large* bottles
*üç **küçük** bira*   three *small* beers

Worth knowing

The people of Turkey are Moslems, but alcoholic drinks are available in most parts of the country. In big hotels and in tourist areas there are bars and cafés where you can buy *viski-soda* (whisky and soda) or *cin-tonik* (gin and tonic). But Turks mostly prefer to do their drinking while they eat – in restaurants. The most popular drinks are *rakı* (a strong aniseed-based spirit), *votka* (vodka), *beyaz şarap* (white wine), *kırmızı şarap* (red wine) and *bira* (beer). Or you may prefer to stick to *su* (water), *meyve suyu* (fruit juice) or *ayran* (yoghurt mixed with salt and water).

The traditional tea-house, *çayhane*, is frequented mostly by men and serves *çay* (tea without milk), *kahve* (Turkish coffee), *gazoz* (fizzy lemonade), *kola* (coke) and *maden suyu* (mineral water). If you order *kahve*, you must say how sweet you want it: *sade* (no sugar), *az şekerli* (with little sugar), *orta* (medium sweet), *şekerli* (sweet). If you want western-style instant coffee rather than Turkish coffee, you must specify that you want *neskafe*. In the summer, these drinks can be found in a *çay bahçesi* (tea-garden). Families and groups of friends often share a pot of tea, which comes on top of a *semaver* (samovar), containing hot water. Smokers can sometimes order a *nargile* (water-pipe). Some tea-gardens serve beer.

Men and women also meet in the *pastane* (patisserie), which sells soft drinks, and where you can eat cakes, sweets and ice-cream – or take them away.

As in many countries in the Near and Middle East, tea and coffee drinking is widespread and almost a ritual. Tea is usually drunk without milk and from small glasses. You can ask for your tea to be *açık* (weak) or *koyu* (strong, *lit.* dark). Turkish tea is grown in the north along the Black Sea and the particular variety is best if brewed slowly – for up to twenty minutes. You'll often see a teapot sitting on top of a larger container with boiling water in to keep the tea hot during the long brew-up. Because of the time it takes, you'll sometimes be told in small cafés *çay yok*. This may not mean they haven't got any, but that it'll be some time before the next lot is ready. If you're doing 'serious' shopping (e.g. a carpet or antique), you'll nearly always be asked by the owner if you want tea or coffee.

Numbers

one	*bir*
two	*iki*
three	*üç*
four	*dört*
five	*beş*
six	*altı*
seven	*yedi*
eight	*sekiz*
nine	*dokuz*
ten	*on*
hundred	*yüz*
thousand	*bin*

N.B. In compound numbers, Turkish does not use 'and'.

105	*yüz beş*
210	*iki yüz on*
1110	*bin yüz on*
5403	*beş bin dört yüz üç*

Exercises

1   What would you say:

(a) to call the waiter's attention?

(b) to order a coffee without sugar?

(c) to ask for the bill?

(d) to say 'thanks'?

2 Translate the following numbers:

(a) yüz on

(b) üç yüz altı

(c) beş yüz

(d) dokuz yüz bir

(e) beş bin beş yüz

(f) on bin

(g) dört bin

3 Take the customer's part in these conversations in a café.

(a) WAITER Buyurun efendim.
    YOU *(Ask if there is any beer?)*
    WAITER Bira yok.
    YOU *(Two coffees, please.)*
    WAITER Kahve nasıl?
    YOU *(One medium, one sweet.)*
    WAITER Hemen efendim.

(b) YOU *(Call the waiter.)*
    WAITER Buyurun efendim.
    YOU *(Order two teas and one instant coffee.)*
    WAITER Sütlü mü, sütsüz mü?
    YOU *(Without milk, please.)*
    WAITER Peki efendim.

(c) YOU *(Call the waiter.)*
    WAITER Buyurun efendim.
    YOU *(Ask for three beers.)*
    WAITER Bira yok efendim.
    YOU *(Ask what they have.)*
    WAITER Kola, fanta, çay, kahve.
    YOU *(Ask if they have fruit juice.)*
    WAITER Var efendim. Neli?
    YOU *(Orange, please.)*
    WAITER Peki efendim.

(d) YOU   *(Call the waiter.)*
   WAITER Buyurun efendim.
   YOU   *(Ask for a bottle of water.)*
   WAITER Büyük mü, küçük mü?
   YOU   *(Small, please.)*
   WAITER Peki.
   YOU   *(Ask if they have Turkish coffee.)*
   WAITER Tabii efendim
   YOU   *(Two medium sweet, please.)*

(e) YOU   *(Call the waiter and ask for the bill.)*
   WAITER İki bin yedi yüz lira efendim.
   YOU   *(Give him the money and tell him to
           keep the change.)*
   WAITER Teşekkür ederim efendim.
   YOU   *(Thank the waiter.)*

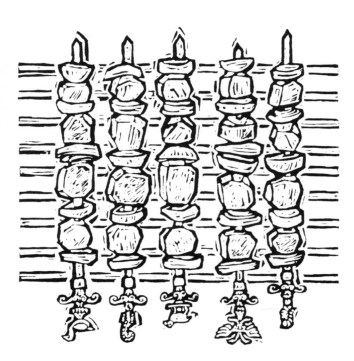

2 Eating out

Key words and phrases

To say 'good morning'
Günaydın.

To say 'good evening'
İyi akşamlar.

To say 'I'd like' or 'I want'
. . . istiyorum.	I'd like . . .
Kahvaltı istiyorum.	I'd like breakfast.

To ask for the menu
Mönü lütfen.

To ask what they have
Ne var?	What have you got?
Izgara ne var?	What grills have you got?

Conversations

1 Ordering breakfast.

WAITER	Günaydın efendim.
MAN	Günaydın, kahvaltı istiyorum[1] lütfen.
WAITER	Peki efendim.
MAN	Yumurta var mı?
WAITER	Var.
MAN	Bir yumurta. Bal var mı?
WAITER	Var efendim.
MAN	Bal ve tereyağı. Peynir var mı?
WAITER	Evet, var.
MAN	Biraz peynir lütfen ve kızarmış ekmek.
WAITER	Yumurta, bal, tereyağı, peynir ve kızarmış ekmek. Zeytin ister misiniz[2]?
MAN	Hayır teşekkür ederim[3].
WAITER	Ne içersiniz? Çay mı, kahve mi?
MAN	Çay lütfen ve biraz süt.
WAITER	Sıcak mı, soğuk mu?
MAN	Soğuk.
WAITER	Hemen efendim.

2 In a restaurant asking for soup.

WAITER Hoş geldiniz, iyi akşamlar.
MAN Hoş bulduk. Çorba var mı?
WAITER Çorba var.
MAN İki domates çorbası.

3 . . . asking what *meze* they have.

MAN Meze ne var[4]?
WAITER Meze pilaki, patlıcan salata, beyaz peynir, ve kavun.
MAN Bir patlıcan salata, bir beyaz peynir, bir kavun.

4 . . . asking what grills they have.

MAN Izgara ne var?
WAITER Izgara döner kebap, şiş kebap, ızgara köfte, biftek ve bonfile var.
MAN Bana[5] bir bonfile lütfen.
WOMAN Bana da[6] bir şiş kebap lütfen.

5 . . . and ordering the drinks.

MAN Bana bir duble rakı.
WOMAN Bana da kırmızı şarap lütfen.

6 . . . and later, the bill.

MAN Garson, lütfen. Hesap.
WAITER Buyurun efendim. Afiyet olsun[7].
MAN Teşekkür ederim.

7 Asking for the menu and ordering a full meal.

WAITER İyi günler[8] efendim, hoş geldiniz.
WOMAN İyi günler, mönü lütfen.
WAITER Buyurun efendim.
WOMAN Teşekkür ederim. Bir mercimek çorbası, bir döner kebap, bir patates tava, bir karışık salata, bir küçük şişe de kırmızı şarap lütfen.
WAITER Bir küçük kırmızı şarap.
WOMAN O kadar.
WAITER Teşekkür ederiz[9].
WOMAN Teşekkür ederim.

8   Asking what vegetable dishes they have.

MAN   Sebze ne var?
WAITER   İmam bayıldı, biber dolması, patlıcan
          kızartması, enginar.
MAN   İmam bayıldı lütfen.

9   Is there any fish?

WOMAN   Balık var mı?
WAITER   Bugün balık yok maalesef, ama ızgaralar
          çok güzel.
WOMAN   Karışık ızgara lütfen.

10   Is there any fruit?

WOMAN   Meyve var mı?
WAITER   Var efendim, üzüm, şeftali, kavun, karpuz.
WOMAN   Şeftali lütfen.
WAITER   Peki efendim.

11   Asking for wine and mineral water . . .

WOMAN   Bir şişe şarap lütfen.
WAITER   Beyaz mı, kırmızı mı?
WOMAN   Beyaz şarap, soğuk lütfen ve maden
          suyu.
WAITER   Bir şişe soğuk beyaz şarap, maden suyu.

12   . . . and would you like something else?

WAITER   Başka bir şey ister misiniz?
WOMAN   Bu kadar yeter, teşekkür ederim.
WAITER   Peki efendim.

Word list

afiyet olsun	bon appétit (see p. 26)
günaydın	good morning
hoş geldiniz	welcome
hoş bulduk	set response to *hoş geldiniz* (*lit.* we find you well)
iyi akşamlar	good evening
iyi günler	good day (*used any time throughout the day*)
teşekkür ederiz	we thank you

bu	this
bugün	today
gün	day
bal	honey
balık	fish
beyaz peynir	white cheese
biber	pepper
biber dolması	stuffed peppers
biftek	steak
bonfile	fillet steak
çorba	soup
döner kebap	doner kebab
domates	tomato
duble	double measure for drinks
ekmek	bread
enginar	artichoke
imam bayıldı	aubergine dish cooked in olive oil (*lit.* the priest has fainted)
ızgara	grill(ed)
ızgara köfte	grilled small hamburgers
kahvaltı	breakfast
karışık salata	mixed salad
karpuz	water melon
kavun	melon
kızarmış ekmek	toasted bread
maden suyu	mineral water
mönü	menu
meyve	fruit
mercimek çorbası	lentil soup
meze	hors d'oeuvres
patates tava	fried potatoes
patlıcan	aubergine
patlıcan kızartması	fried aubergine
peynir	cheese
pilaki	white beans cooked in sauce
salata	salad
sebze	vegetable
şeftali	peach
şiş kebap	lamb pieces grilled on skewers
tereyağı	butter
üzüm	grapes
yumurta	egg
zeytin	olive
başka	other, else
bir şey	something, a thing
biraz	a little
bu kadar	this much

çok	very, a lot
maalesef	unfortunately
o kadar	that much
yeter	enough (it suffices)
beyaz	white
güzel	beautiful, nice
kırmızı	red
sıcak	hot
soğuk	cold
ama	but
bana	to me, for me
başka bir şey?	anything else?
evet	yes
hayır	no
ister misiniz?	would you like?
istiyorum	I want/would like
ve	and

Explanations

1 İstiyorum

İstiyorum means 'I'd like' or 'I want':

Çay istiyorum.	I'd like tea.
Bir bira istiyorum.	I'd like a beer.
Çorba istiyorum.	I'd like soup.

2 When someone else asks you 'Would you like
. . .?', it's:

Zeytin ister misiniz?	Would you like olives?
Şeker ister misiniz?	Do you want sugar?

3 'Yes/No, thank you'

Evet teşekkür ederim.	Yes, thank you.
Hayır teşekkür ederim.	No, thank you.

4 When ordering a meal, you can ask 'What
(grills/soup/vegetables) have you got?':

Izgara ne var?	What grills have you got?
Çorba ne var?	What soup have you got?
Sebze ne var?	What vegetables have you got?

Ne? means 'what?'.

If you want to keep things really simple, however,
you can just ask for the menu:

Mönü lütfen.	The menu please.

5 *Bana*

Bana means 'for me' when you're ordering a meal in company:
Bana döner kebap. A doner kebab for me/I'll have a doner kebab.

6 *De/da*

De (or *da*, depending on the vowel harmony) means 'too', 'and . . . as well':

Çay soğuk, kahve de soğuk.	The tea's cold and the coffee's cold as well.
Bana da kırmızı şarap.	And red wine for me.

7 *Afiyet olsun*

Afiyet olsun means 'may it do you good'. It's not quite the same as the French *bon appétit* because, as well as saying it before you start your meal, the waiter will often say it as you pay the bill or as you leave.

8 *İyi günler*

İyi günler means 'good day'. It can be said all through the day until early evening as a greeting and also when you take leave of someone.

9 *Teşekkür ederiz*

Teşekkür ederiz means 'we thank you'. You'll hear it instead of *teşekkür ederim* when a shopkeeper or waiter is speaking on behalf of the shop or restaurant. You can say it when you're speaking for a group – i.e. two or more of you in a restaurant. The most usual reply to any form of thanks is *bir şey değil* ('it's nothing').

Worth knowing

Restaurants

The traditional, simple *lokanta* or *restoran* opens early in the morning – around seven o'clock – for breakfast and closes early to mid-evening. It is usually *içkisiz*: that is, alcohol is not available (although some restaurants do serve *bira* – beer). A basic breakfast is served of *çorba* (soup), *süt* (hot milk) and *yoğurt*. *Peynir* (cheese) may also be available. The full range of *lokanta yemeği* (restaurant food) is available at lunch-time – from around 12.00 onwards. Most of the dishes are meat or vegetables cooked in meat stock and are kept warm, usually in the front of the restaurant, until the customer selects what he or she wants. You can usually indicate to the waiter or chef what you want. Strict vegetarians may have some difficulty in these restaurants finding dishes that have not been cooked in meat stock. *Ekmek* (bread) is provided automatically.

Another type of restaurant is the *kebapçı* (kebab house). The basic kebabs are *döner kebap, şiş kebap* (small pieces of lamb grilled on skewers) and *şiş köfte* (mince grilled on skewers). *Şiş köfte* can be cooked either with hot spices (*acılı*) or without (*acısız*). *Acılı şiş köfte* is also called *Adana kebabı* and can be very hot. Kebabs may be served *sade* (by themselves), *pideli* (on flat bread), *salçalı* (with tomato sauce) or *yoğurtlu* (with yoghurt).

An elaborate form of *kebapçı* in large cities is the *et lokantası* (meat restaurant), where families go out to gorge themselves on a wide variety of grills. Spitted chicken (*piliç*) may be available: you can order *yarım piliç* (half a chicken), either *pilavlı* (with rice) or *bulgurlu* (with cracked wheat).

Restaurants that cater for people who are eating out for pleasure rather than necessity are usually *içkili* (they serve alcohol). The most popular drink is *rakı*, and this is often drunk with a selection of different types of *meze* (hors d'oeuvres – although you may not want anything more to eat). Your *rakı* will arrive with a separate glass (or jug) of water so you may dilute it to taste. Afterwards, kebabs may be served and there are usually vegetables available. These are called *zeytinyağlı* (cooked with olive oil rather than meat stock) and are served cold. *Salata* (salad) is also eaten. On the coast, and in Ankara, there are fish restaurants. Fish is usually sold by weight, and you can often choose the fish you want before it is cooked. You may ask for it *tava* (fried), *ızgara* (grilled), *buğulama* (steamed) or *kiremitte* (baked on a tile in the oven). *Rakı* is the normal drink with fish.

Turkey is not a country of late eaters. *İçkisiz* restaurants often close around 8.30 p.m. *İçkili* restaurants usually stay open until 11 p.m. or midnight, but it is sensible not to arrive much after 9.30. In the fasting month of *Ramazan* (the dates change each year), strict Moslems neither eat nor drink during daylight hours. In more conservative parts of the country, restaurants and tea-houses do not operate during the day. There is a frantic rush to the restaurants at dusk, and if you do not eat immediately it is dark, there may be nothing left.

Other types of restaurant and fast food: increasingly popular is the *pideci*, a restaurant with a pizza-style oven. *Pide* (flat bread) is baked *peynirli* (with cheese) or *kıymalı* (with mince). *Lahmacun* is a thin pancake baked in the oven, covered with mince, tomatoes and onions. The *büfe* is a snack-bar that sells *sandöviç* (sandwiches) and cold drinks. *Döner kebap* is served in sandwiches. *Tost* is not toast (which is *kızarmış ekmek*), but a toasted sandwich.

Domuz eti (pork) is not eaten by Moslems and is unavailable except in a few luxury establishments in the large cities. It is not tactful to ask for it.

Tipping: ten per cent is usual in restaurants.

Exercises

1 How would you greet people

(a) first thing in the morning?

(b) in the evening?

(c) at any other time of day?

2 Take the customer's part in these conversations in a restaurant.

(a) WAITER Buyurun efendim.
    YOU *(Say you want breakfast.)*
    WAITER Peki efendim.
    YOU *(Order butter, honey, two eggs and toasted bread.)*
    WAITER Ne içersiniz?
    YOU *(Ask for tea and a little milk.)*

(b) WAITER Hoş geldiniz.
    YOU *(Respond to the welcome and ask for the menu.)*
    WAITER Buyurun efendim.
    YOU *(Order a mixed grill, fried potatoes and aubergine salad.)*
    WAITER Ne içersiniz?
    YOU *(Ask if they have wine.)*
    WAITER Şarap var. Beyaz mı, kırmızı mı?
    YOU *(A small bottle of red wine, please.)*
    WAITER Peki efendim.

(c) WAITER İyi akşamlar efendim, buyurun.
    YOU *(Respond to the waiter and ask what grills they have.)*
    WAITER Izgara köfte, şiş kebap, döner kebap.
    YOU *(Order grilled hamburgers, fried potatoes and a mixed salad.)*
    WAITER Başka?
    YOU *(Say that that is enough.)*

3 Choose the odd one out in the following sentences.

(a) Tereyağı, bal, iki yumurta, kızarmış ekmek, döner kebap.

(b) Izgara köfte, biftek, portakal, bonfile, şiş kebap.

(c) Pilaki, beyaz peynir, kavun, kırmızı şarap, patlıcan salatası.

(d) Bira, şarap, çay, rakı.

3 Shopping

Key words and phrases

To ask how much something is
Şeftali ne kadar? How much are the peaches?
Bu cezve kaç lira? How many lira is this coffee pot?

To say 'half a kilo'
Yarım kilo

To say 'anything else?'
Başka ne?

To say 'that's all'.
Bu kadar.

To ask 'how much does it all come to?'
Hepsi ne kadar?

To say 'goodbye'
Allahaısmarladık. (said by person leaving)
Güle güle. (said by person staying behind)

To say 'thanks' casually . . .
Sağol/Sağolun.

. . . and the reply
Bir şey değil. It's nothing.

Conversations

1 Buying some fruit in the street market: half a kilo of peaches and half of grapes.

SHOPPER	İyi günler.
STALLHOLDER	İyi günler efendim.
SHOPPER	Yarım kilo¹ şeftali.
STALLHOLDER	Evet.
SHOPPER	Yarım kilo üzüm.
STALLHOLDER	Evet.

2 How much are the apples?

SHOPPER	Elma kaç lira[2]?
STALLHOLDER	Elma dört yüz.
SHOPPER	Yarım kilo da elma.
STALLHOLDER	Evet.

3 How much is it all?

SHOPPER	Hepsi ne kadar?
STALLHOLDER	Bin beş yüz lira.
SHOPPER	Buyurun.
STALLHOLDER	Teşekkür ederiz.
SHOPPER	İyi günler.
STALLHOLDER	İyi günler.

4 In a supermarket a shopper buys a kilo of tomatoes, six eggs and Turkish coffee.

WOMAN	Günaydın.
SHOPKEEPER	Buyurun.
WOMAN	Bir kilo domates lütfen.
SHOPKEEPER	Yok.
WOMAN	Altı yumurta.
SHOPKEEPER	Var.
WOMAN	Türk kahvesi var mı?
SHOPKEEPER	Var.
WOMAN	Yüz gram Türk kahvesi lütfen.

5 And how much does it all come to?

WOMAN	Hepsi ne kadar?
SHOPKEEPER	Altı yüz yumurta, bin dört yüz kahve, iki bin.
WOMAN	Tamam, buyurun. Teşekkürler.
SHOPKEEPER	İyi günler.
WOMAN	Allahaısmarladık.
SHOPKEEPER	Güle güle.

6 Now the grocer's, for white cheese, butter and bread.

WOMAN	İyi günler.
SHOPKEEPER	İyi günler efendim, hoş geldiniz.
WOMAN	İki yüz gram beyaz peynir lütfen.
SHOPKEEPER	Başka ne?
WOMAN	Bir küçük paket tereyağı, bir ekmek.

SHOPKEEPER	Olur efendim, hemen.
WOMAN	Ne kadar?
SHOPKEEPER	Dokuz yüz elli, bin iki yüz elli, bir ekmek iki yüz . . . iki bin dört yüz.
WOMAN	Peki buyurun.
SHOPKEEPER	Teşekkür ederiz.
WOMAN	Allahaısmarladık.
SHOPKEEPER	Güle güle.

7 Now a large bottle of water and two bottles of beer.

WOMAN	İyi günler.
ASSISTANT	İyi günler efendim, buyurun.
WOMAN	Bir büyük şişe su, iki şişe bira lütfen. (*He serves her.*) Hepsi ne kadar?
ASSISTANT	Hepsi bin sekiz yüz lira efendim.
WOMAN	Buyurun.
ASSISTANT	Teşekkür ederim.

8 . . . and getting the change from a 10,000 lira note.

ASSISTANT	Bin sekiz yüz, bin dokuz yüz, iki bin, üç bin, dört bin, beş bin, beş te bu, on bin.
WOMAN	Çok teşekkürler.
ASSISTANT	Ben[3] teşekkür ederim.
WOMAN	İyi günler.
ASSISTANT	İyi günler efendim.

9 Buying a bottle of good red wine.

WOMAN	Merhaba.
ASSISTANT	Merhaba.
WOMAN	Bir şişe iyi şarap istiyorum.
ASSISTANT	Kırmızı mı beyaz mı?
WOMAN	Kırmızı lütfen.
ASSISTANT	Kırmızı.

10 Buying souvenirs from an antique dealer: a plate and a coffee pot.

WOMAN	Merhaba.
DEALER	Merhaba, buyurun.
WOMAN	Bu[4] tabak ne kadar?

DEALER	Yirmi beş bin lira.
WOMAN	Peki, bu?
DEALER	Kırk bin lira.
WOMAN	Bu cezve ne kadar?
DEALER	Büyük beş bin, küçük üç bin.
WOMAN	Teşekkür ederim.
DEALER	Bir şey değil.

11 Buying a bag in a leather shop.

ASSISTANT	Hoş geldiniz.
WOMAN	İyi günler.
ASSISTANT	Buyurun.
WOMAN	Bir çanta istiyorum.
ASSISTANT	Ne renk?
WOMAN	Siyah lütfen.
ASSISTANT	Modeller bunlar.
WOMAN	(*choosing one*) Bu ne kadar?
ASSISTANT	Yüz yirmi bin.

12 Is there a cheaper one?

WOMAN	Daha ucuz[5] var mı?
ASSISTANT	Var (*pointing to others*).
WOMAN	Bu ne kadar?
ASSISTANT	Seksen altı bin.
WOMAN	Çok güzel, iyi, peki.
ASSISTANT	Teşekkürler.
WOMAN	Teşekkürler.

13 Buying a map of Istanbul in a bookshop.

BOOKSELLER	Günaydın.
WOMAN	Günaydın. Bu İstanbul haritası ne kadar?
BOOKSELLER	Dört bin lira.
WOMAN	İyi, peki.

14 Buying ten stamps for postcards to Britain.

TOURIST	Günaydın.
CLERK	Günaydın.
TOURIST	İngiltere'ye posta kartı kaç lira?
CLERK	Üç yüz lira.
TOURIST	On pul lütfen.
CLERK	Buyurun. Üç bin lira.
TOURIST	Buyurun, teşekkür ederim.

Word list

elma	apple
ben	I
merhaba	hello
olur	all right
daha	more
ucuz	cheap
daha ucuz	cheaper
elli	fifty
hepsi	all, all of it/them
kaç?	how many/how much?
kaç lira?	how many lira?
kırk	forty
ne kadar?	how much?
seksen	eighty
yarım	half
yirmi	twenty
çok	very, much, a lot of
ne renk?	what colour?
renk	colour
siyah	black
bu	this
bunlar	these ones
cezve	special pot for making Turkish coffee
çanta	bag
harita	map
İstanbul haritası	map of Istanbul
model	style, model
paket	packet
posta kartı	postcard
pul	stamp
tabak	plate
İngiltere	England
İngiltere'ye	*to England*

Explanations

1 To buy things by weight

bir kilo elma	a kilo of apples
iki kilo şeftali	two kilos of peaches
yarım kilo üzüm	half a kilo of grapes

This is very simple in Turkish: the noun stays in the singular (because it follows a number – see page 16), and you don't need to translate the word 'of'.

Note, however, that for 1½, 2½ etc. you don't say *yarım* but *buçuk*:

bir buçuk kilo elma   a kilo and a half of apples
bir buçuk gün   a day and a half

2 To ask the price of something

There are three possible ways of doing this in Turkish:

Kaça? How much?
Ne kadar? How much?
Kaç lira? How many lira?

They all come at the end of the question:

Şeftali { *kaça?*
          kaç lira?
          ne kadar? }

Note: *kaç?* with a noun means 'how much?' or 'how many?':

Kaç gün? How many days?
Kaç para? How much money?

3 *Ben*

Ben means 'I'. It is emphatic in phrases like:
Ben teşekkür ederim   I thank you

4 *Bu*

Bu means 'this' or 'this one':
Bu cezve kaç lira?   How much is this coffee pot?
Bu kaç lira?   How much is this?

5 *Daha*

Daha means 'more' or '-er':
daha ucuz   cheaper
daha güzel   nicer/more beautiful

'Expensive' is *pahalı*, so if you think an item is too dear you can say: *bu çok pahalı* ('this is very expensive').

Worth knowing

Bargaining is an accepted practice when buying valuable items like a carpet, a leather jacket or a piece of jewellery, so you can always start off by offering less than the asking price. Some of the things most commonly bought by visitors to Turkey are:

tabak	plate
cezve	Turkish coffee pot
şiş	meat skewer
halı	carpet
kilim	flat-weave rug
fincan	cup
çanta	bag
deri ceket	leather jacket
bakır	copper

Some shops and all banks close for the lunch hour which may be from 12 or 12.30 p.m. to 1.30 or 2 p.m.

To use a public pay phone you will need a metal token called a *jeton*. There are different sizes of *jeton* for local and international calls. There are also some public telephones which work on phonecards.

More numbers

20	*yirmi*
30	*otuz*
40	*kırk*
50	*elli*
60	*altmış*
70	*yetmiş*
80	*seksen*
90	*doksan*

And there is no word for 'and' in compound numbers.

23	*yirmi üç*
48	*kırk sekiz*
169	*yüz altmış dokuz*
3597	*üç bin beş yüz doksan yedi*

In dates, the year is read just like any number, e.g. 1999 is *bin dokuz yüz doksan dokuz*.

Telephone numbers are read out in groups of two digits at a time, e.g. a number in four digits with a four-digit code like 1931 2364 is *on dokuz, otuz bir, yirmi üç, altmış dört*. For simplicity, however, you can just say each number separately.

Exercises

1   You are in a shop. Ask for the following:

(a) half a kilo of tomatoes

(b) a kilo of grapes

(c) four eggs

(d) three hundred grams of white cheese

(e) how much it all comes to

2   Ask the price of the following:

(a) this large plate

(b) the black bag

(c) the small coffee pot

(d) half a kilo of apples

(e) one bottle of red wine

3   What is the price if the shopkeeper says:

(a) üç bin altı yüz elli

(b) iki yüz seksen

(c) bin iki yüz elli

(d) yirmi dokuz bin yedi yüz kırk

(e) yüz elli bin sekiz yüz on beş

4   Take the customer's part in this dialogue.

SHOPKEEPER   İyi günler efendim. Buyurun.
YOU   *(How much is this plate?)*
SHOPKEEPER   Yirmi üç bin lira.
YOU   *(Very nice, but a little expensive.)*

SHOPKEEPER	Bu daha ucuz.
YOU	*(How much?)*
SHOPKEEPER	On sekiz bin lira.
YOU	*(Fine, OK. And what do you say as you hand the money over?)*
SHOPKEEPER	Teşekkürler. Güle güle.
YOU	*(Goodbye.)*

4 Visiting sites

Key words and phrases

To say 'excuse me'
Affedersiniz.

To ask 'where is the beach?'
Plaj nerede?

To ask 'is it open?'
Açık mı?

To ask 'when will it open?'
Ne zaman açılır?

Conversations

In Istanbul you can cross from Europe to Asia and vice versa by the bridges or on the steamer. One of the places you might land on the European side is Sirkeci.

1 Where does the boat to Sirkeci leave from?

VISITOR	Sirkeci'ye[1] vapur nereden[2]?
PASSER-BY	Sağ taraftan.
VISITOR	Sağ taraftan. Teşekkürler.

2 Is this the Sirkeci boat?

VISITOR	Sirkeci vapuru bu mu?
PASSER-BY	Evet efendim, bu.
VISITOR	Teşekkür ederim.
PASSER-BY	Bir şey değil efendim.

3 Where is Topkapi Palace?

VISITOR	Affedersiniz, Topkapı Sarayı nerede[3]?
PASSER-BY	Az ileride, sağda karşıda.
VISITOR	Teşekkür ederim.
PASSER-BY	Bir şey değil.

4 ... go straight on, it is 400 metres further on.

VISITOR   Affedersiniz, Topkapı Sarayı nerede?
PASSER-BY Düz gidin, dört yüz metre sonra[4].
VISITOR   Teşekkür ederim.
PASSER-BY Bir şey değil.

5 How much is the entrance fee?

VISITOR   Giriş ne kadar?
OFFICIAL   Bin lira.
VISITOR   İki bilet lütfen.
OFFICIAL   Buyurun.
VISITOR   Teşekkürler.
OFFICIAL   Bir şey değil.

6 Is there a bus to Sultan Ahmet?

VISITOR   Affedersiniz, Sultan Ahmed'e otobüs
             var mı?
PASSER-BY Tabii var.
VISITOR   Nerede?
PASSER-BY Orada.

7 When is the museum open?

VISITOR   Affedersiniz, müze ne zaman[5] açık?
OFFICIAL   Saat dokuzdan beşe kadar[6].
VISITOR   Hergün mü?
OFFICIAL   Salı hariç hergün.
VISITOR   Teşekkür ederim, iyi günler.
OFFICIAL   İyi günler.

8 Is the mosque open?

VISITOR   Affedersiniz, cami açık mı?
OFFICIAL   Hayır, kapalı.

9 When will it open?

VISITOR   Ne zaman açılır?
PASSER-BY İkide.
VISITOR   Teşekkür ederim.
PASSER-BY Bir şey değil.

10 Where is the entrance of the mosque?

VISITOR   Affedersiniz, cami girişi nerede?
OFFICIAL   Solda.

VISITOR	Giriş ne kadar?
OFFICIAL	Giriş serbest.
VISITOR	Teşekkürler.
OFFICIAL	Bir şey değil.

11 I want to go to the town centre, where is the bus-stop?

WOMAN	Affedersiniz, şehir merkezine gitmek istiyorum[7], otobüs durağı nerede?
MAN	Orada, yüz metre ileride.
WOMAN	Peki, teşekkürler.
MAN	Bir şey değil.
WOMAN	İyi günler.
MAN	İyi günler.

12 Where is the beach?

WOMAN	Affedersiniz, plaj nerede?
MAN	Bu tarafta.
WOMAN	Uzak mı?

. . . five minutes on foot.

MAN	Yürüyerek[8] beş dakika.
WOMAN	Teşekkür ederim.
MAN	Bir şey değil.
WOMAN	İyi günler.
MAN	İyi günler.

13 Asking for an address: where is Ethem Efendi Road?

WOMAN	Affedersiniz, Ethem Efendi Caddesi nerede?
MAN	Düz gidin, solda ikinci[9] cadde.
WOMAN	Teşekkür ederim. İyi günler.
MAN	İyi günler.

Word list

düz	straight on
ileride	further on
karşıda	opposite
ne zaman?	when?
ne zaman açılır?	when will it open?
nerede?	where?
nereden?	from where?

orada	there
sağ	right
sağ taraftan	from the right-hand side
sol	left
solda	on the left
taraf	side
bilet	ticket
cadde	road, street
cami	mosque
Ethem Efendi Caddesi	Ethem Efendi Road
giriş	entry, entrance
metre	metre
merkez	centre
müze	museum
otobüs	bus, coach
otobüs durağı	bus stop
plaj	beach
saray	palace
şehir	city, town
şehir merkezi	town centre
vapur	boat, ferry
açık	open
affedersiniz	excuse me
gidin	go (formal)
hariç	except
hergün	every day
ikinci	second
kapalı	closed
Salı	Tuesday
serbest	free, no charge
uzak	far, far away
yürüyerek	on foot

Explanations

1 *Nereye?* To where?

If you want to say 'to' a specific place, add *-e* or *-a*
(or *-ye/-ya* after a vowel) to the relevant word:

İstanbul'a	to Istanbul
İzmir'e	to Izmir
müzeye	to the museum
Londra'ya	to London
Ankara'ya otobüs var mı?	Is there a bus to Ankara?
Plaja otobüs var mı?	Is there a bus to the beach?

Note the apostrophe with proper nouns.

2 *Nereden?* From where?

Otobüs nereden kalkıyor? Where does the bus leave from?

To say 'from' a specific place, add the ending *-den* (or *-dan, -ten, -tan*) to the basic word:

*İstanbul'**dan*** from Istanbul
*İzmir'**den*** from Izmir
*İstanbul'**dan** İzmir'**e** gidiyorum* I am going from Istanbul to Izmir

3 *Nerede?* Where?

Plaj nerede? Where is the beach?
Şehir merkezi nerede? Where is the town centre?

Possible answers to *. . . nerede?* are:
burada here
orada there
gidin go
düz straight on
sağda on the right
solda on the left
ileride further on

-de (or *-da, -te, -ta*) can be tagged on to the end of a word to mean 'in, on, at':

*İstanbul'**da*** in Istanbul
*İzmir'**de*** in Izmir
*masa**da*** on the table
*kahve**de** şeker yok* there's no sugar in the coffee

4 *Sonra* Later, afterwards, further on

*dört yüz metre **sonra*** 400 metres further on
*iki saat **sonra*** two hours later (i.e. in two hours' time)
*beş gün **sonra*** five days later

5 *Ne zaman?* When?

*Müze **ne zaman** açık?* When is the museum open?
*Otobüs **ne zaman** kalkıyor?* When does the bus leave?
*Ayşe İstanbul'a **ne zaman** gidiyor?* When is Ayşe going to Istanbul?

6 To tell the time

saat iki   two o'clock
saat dokuz   nine o'clock
saat on   ten o'clock

-*den (or* -*dan)...* -*e kadar*   from...until...
Müze ne zaman açık?   When is the museum open?
Saat dokuzdan beşe kadar.   From 9 o'clock until 5.

7 *Gitmek istiyorum*   I want to go

To say you want to do something, you use the verb
with -*mek* (or -*mak*) followed by *istiyorum* (I want):
Almak istiyorum.   I want to buy.
Çanta almak istiyorum.   I want to buy a bag.
İstanbul'a gitmek istiyorum.   I want to go to
Istanbul.

8 *Yürüyerek*   On foot (lit. 'by walking')

Plaja yürüyerek gitmek istiyorum. I want to go to the
beach on foot.

9 Ordinal numbers (first, second...)

Add -*inci* (-*üncü* etc.) to the cardinal number (one,
two... etc.):
birinci   first
ikinci   second
üçüncü   third
dördüncü   fourth
beşinci   fifth
yüzüncü   hundredth

Worth knowing

Istanbul

Istanbul is one of the great cities of the world and
any visitor should be equipped with a good guide
book that gives the history and background of the
best places to visit.

In addition to mosques, palaces, churches and
museums, a special attraction of Istanbul is that it
spans two continents, Europe and Asia, divided by
the narrow channel of the Bosphorus. There are

bridges, but a spectacular way to cross is by the large crowded steamers that carry thousands of people every day. If you cross at dusk you will see the sun set behind the skyline of mosques and minarets on the European side.

Visiting mosques

All mosques in Turkey can be visited by non-Moslems. Behave rather as if you are visiting a cathedral in Britain. It is advisable not to enter mosques during prayer-times. Women are expected to cover their heads – and it is sensible to take a headscarf and avoid shorts, short skirts and short sleeves if you are planning to visit mosques. Men, too, should dress soberly, and both men and women should wear socks or stockings.

At the entrance to the mosque there is usually a slightly raised platform, often covered in linoleum or matting. Step out of your shoes on to the platform – being careful neither to put your stockinged feet on the dirty pavement nor your shoes on the platform or on the carpets inside the mosque. Pick up your shoes, carry them with you into the mosque and, together with any luggage you are carrying, place them, sole to sole, on the racks provided. Inside the mosque, move around quietly, without talking loudly or otherwise disturbing worshippers. Avoid walking directly in front of people who are praying, and do not take photographs unless you have arranged permission in advance. There is usually an alms-box in the mosque and it is courteous to place an offering in it. You will not be charged to enter mosques.

Public lavatories

Public lavatories (*tuvalet, helâ* or *yüznumara*) are sometimes marked *Baylar* (Gents) and *Bayanlar* (Ladies) or *Erkek* (Men) and *Kadın* (Women). They may also be designated by the sign O O. Lavatories are often to be found in the main squares of towns, at bus and railway stations, and in mosque courtyards. You are expected to pay a small fee (usually indicated on a notice) on your way out.

Exercises

1 Ask where the following are:

(a) Bağdat Street
(b) the mosque
(c) the mosque entrance
(d) the bus-stop
(e) the museum

2 Translate the following directions:

(a) A little further on.
(b) It is on the right.
(c) Third road on the left.
(d) Go straight on.
(e) 200 metres further on.

3 You want to see the mosque.

(a) Ask if the mosque is open.
(b) Ask when it will be open.
(c) Ask how much the entrance fee is.
(d) Ask where the entrance is.

4 The following are all to do with time. What do they mean?

(a) saat üç
(b) saat sekiz
(c) saat dokuzdan bire kadar
(d) saat üçe kadar
(e) üç saat sonra
(f) dört gün sonra
(g) saat ondan sekize kadar

5 You want to get to the beach. Say:

(a) Excuse me, I want to go to the beach.

(b) Where is the beach?

(c) Is there a bus to the beach?

(d) Is it far?

(e) Thank you.

6 You are talking to a guide outside a museum.

YOU *(Excuse me. When is the museum open?)*
GUIDE Saat dokuzdan beşe kadar.
YOU *(Every day?)*
GUIDE Salı hariç hergün.
YOU *(How much is the entrance fee?)*
GUIDE İki bin lira.
YOU *(Where is the entrance?)*
GUIDE Orada.
YOU *(Thank you. Goodbye.)*
GUIDE Güle güle.

Ayasofya (The Mosque of Saint Sophia, Istanbul)

5 Travelling

Key words and phrases

To ask 'What's the time?'
Saat kaç?
Saat iki   It's two o'clock

To ask 'At what time?'
Saat kaçta?
Saat ikide   At two o'clock

To ask 'Which day?'
Hangi gün?

To ask how to get somewhere
Nasıl giderim?

To ask how long it will take
Ne kadar sürer?

To say 'I don't know'
Bilmiyorum

Conversations

1   Asking about a flight from Istanbul to Antalya for tomorrow.

TOURIST	İyi günler.
TRAVEL AGENT	İyi günler.
TOURIST	Antalya'ya uçak var mı?
TRAVEL AGENT	Var. Hangi[1] gün için[2]?
TOURIST	Yarın için.
TRAVEL AGENT	Bir dakika *(checks in airline timetable)*. İki uçak var. Birinci uçak saat yedi onbeşte[3], ikinci uçak saat yirmi onbeşte.

2 Buying a one-way ticket.

TOURIST	Bilet kaç lira?
TRAVEL AGENT	Gidiş mi, gidiş dönüş mü?
TOURIST	Gidiş.
TRAVEL AGENT	Altmış beş bin lira.
TOURIST	Peki, teşekkür ederim.
TRAVEL AGENT	Bir şey değil.
TOURIST	İyi günler.
TRAVEL AGENT	İyi günler.

3 When is the bus to Ephesus?

TOURIST	Affedersiniz, Efes'e otobüs saat kaçta?
TRAVEL AGENT	Saat dokuzda.
TOURIST	Dokuzda mı?
TRAVEL AGENT	Evet, dokuzda.
TOURIST	Peki, teşekkürler.
TRAVEL AGENT	Bir şey değil.
TOURIST	Allahaısmarladık.
TRAVEL AGENT	İyi günler, güle güle.

4 How can I get to the airport?

TOURIST	Affedersiniz, havaalanına gitmek istiyorum. Nasıl giderim[4]?
TRAVEL AGENT	Buraya çok uzak, en[5] iyisi taksiyle[6] gitmek.
TOURIST	Taksi ne kadar?
TRAVEL AGENT	Maalesef bilmiyorum.
TOURIST	Peki, teşekkürler.
TRAVEL AGENT	İyi günler.
TOURIST	İyi günler.

5 What's the time?

WOMAN	Affedersiniz, saat kaç?
PASSER-BY	Saat dört.
WOMAN	Teşekkür ederim.
PASSER-BY	Bir şey değil.

6 Buying a return ticket to Ankara.

TRAVELLER   Affedersiniz, Ankara'ya tren saat kaçta?
TICKET CLERK   Ankara'ya hergün saat on üç otuzda Mavi Tren var.
TRAVELLER   Bir bilet lütfen.
TICKET CLERK   Gidiş mi?
TRAVELLER   Gidiş dönüş lütfen.
TICKET CLERK   Buyurun. On altı bin altı yüz lira.
TRAVELLER   Buyurun . . .

7 And how long will it take?

TRAVELLER   Ne kadar sürer?
TICKET CLERK   Sekiz saat.
TRAVELLER   Peki, teşekkür ederim. İyi günler.
TICKET CLERK   Güle güle.

8 Where is the Ankara train?

TRAVELLER   Affedersiniz, Ankara'ya tren nerede?
PORTER   Dördüncü platformda.
TRAVELLER   Teşekkürler.
PORTER   Bir şey değil.

9 Booking a room at a hotel.

RECEPTIONIST   İyi akşamlar.
WOMAN   Boş oda var mı[7]?
RECEPTIONIST   Kaç kişi için?
WOMAN   İki kişi için.
RECEPTIONIST   Kaç gece için?
WOMAN   Bir gece için.
RECEPTIONIST   Bir dakika. *(He checks in register)* Var.

10 With or without a bath?

RECEPTIONIST   Banyolu mu, banyosuz mu?
WOMAN   Banyolu kaç lira?
RECEPTIONIST   Banyolu yetmiş üç bin lira.
WOMAN   İyi, peki.
RECEPTIONIST   Pasaportunuz lütfen.
WOMAN   Buyurun.
RECEPTIONIST   Teşekkür ederim.

Word list

havaalanı	airport
Mavi Tren	the Blue Train
pasaport	passport
peron/platform	platform
taksi	taxi
tren	train
uçak	aeroplane
boş	vacant, empty
banyo	bath/bathroom
buraya	to here
dakika	minute
en	most, -est
en iyisi	the best, best of all
gece	night
gidiş	one-way, single
gidiş dönüş	return
için	for
kişi	person, people
oda	room
yarın	tomorrow

Explanations

1 *Hangi*

Hangi means 'which?' and is placed before the noun:

Hangi gün? Which day?

Hangi tren Ankara'ya gidiyor? Which train goes to Ankara?

Hangi çanta daha ucuz? Which bag is cheaper?

2 *İçin*

İçin means 'for':

Yarın için *bilet var mı?* Is there a ticket *for* tomorrow?

İstanbul için *bir bilet istiyorum* I want a ticket *for* Istanbul

In hotels you will be asked:

Kaç kişi için? For how many people?

Kaç gece için? For how many nights?

You answer as appropriate:
İki kişi için   For two people
Bir gece için   For one night
Note: *için* is placed at the end of the phrase.

3   *Saat kaçta?*

Saat kaçta? means 'at what time?' In the answer,
you put -*de* (or -*da, -te, -ta*) after the time:
saat beşte   at five o'clock
beşte   at five
beş buçukta   at half-past five
beş otuzda   at 5.30
Buçuk is used for the half hour, but 'at 12.30' is
yarımda (and not *on iki buçukta*).

In timetables, the 24-hour clock is normally used:
Ankara'ya tren on üç otuzda   The train to Ankara
is at 13.30
Londra'ya uçak saat yirmide   The plane to
London is at 20.00

4   How do I go to . . .?

'I go' is   *giderim.*
'How do I go . . .?'   *Nasıl giderim?*
So:
Antalya'ya nasıl giderim?   How do I get to
Antalya?

5   *En*

En before an adjective means 'most' or '-est';
ucuz   cheap   *daha ucuz*   cheaper
en ucuz   cheapest
en güzel tabak   the nicest plate
en ucuz bilet   the cheapest ticket
en iyi   the best
en iyisi   the best of all

6 To say 'with' or 'by', add *-yle* (or *-yla, -le, -la*) to the word:

taksiyle   by taxi
trenle   by train
uçakla   by plane
otobüsle   by bus
Ankara'ya trenle gitmek istiyorum   I want to go to Ankara by train

7 To book a hotel room, ask for a 'vacant' room:
Boş oda var mı?

Worth knowing

Travel in Turkey
The domestic flights of THY – *Türk Hava Yolları* (Turkish Air Lines) – are a good way to reach the more distant parts of the country. Tickets can be bought at the *havaalanı* (airport) or at THY offices in the city centres. There is a bus service to the airports.

Train tickets are sold at railway stations *(istasyon).* You can buy a *gidiş* (one-way) or *gidiş-dönüs bileti* (return ticket). Inter-city bus services are run by private companies, and competition keeps prices down. Buses are normally quicker than the train. Some bus companies have offices in the city centres, but normally you go to the bus station *(otogar* or *garajlar).*

Getting a seat on any form of public transport can be very difficult at the beginning and end of public holidays. The greatest problems occur during the Moslem Feast of Sacrifice *(Kurban Bayramı),* when there is a shortage of buses, as a large number are removed from circulation to take pilgrims to Mecca.

For shorter distances, between villages and small towns, you can travel by *minibüs* or *dolmuş* (a shared taxi following a particular route; each passenger pays a fixed rate). There are also *dolmuş* in some large cities. In Istanbul they tend to be huge American saloon cars of the 1940s and 1950s and take up to about eight passengers.

In Istanbul you cross the Bosphorus by *vapur* (ferry): you have to buy a special *jeton* (metal token) at the *gişe* (ticket office). A car ferry is called *feribot*.

Hitch-hiking is not normal practice in Turkey and is not advisable, certainly not for women. Men who do hitch-hike should offer the driver money equivalent to the bus fare for the journey they have made. The driver may or may not accept it.

In the big cities, tickets for the municipal buses have to be bought in advance from offices at important route centres.

Hotels

Because of the rapid depreciation of the Turkish lira in recent years, prices in the more expensive hotels are fixed in US dollars. You pay in lira – but the amount varies, depending on the value of the dollar against the lira. When you register, it is worth enquiring if the price includes breakfast: *kahvaltı dahil mi?*

Finding a hotel can be a problem, particularly during the tourist season and during the two major Moslem festivals. Hotel rooms are also hard to come by in Izmir in late August/early September, during the Izmir Industrial Fair, and in Bursa at New Year. And the Greek Orthodox Easter (which sometimes, but not always, coincides with Easter in Britain) is an occasion for tens of thousands of Greek tourists to visit Istanbul: finding a hotel room can be extremely difficult then. Good hotels in Istanbul can be expensive: if you plan to spend some time there, it is advisable to arrange accommodation through a travel agent in Britain.

In more remote parts of Turkey, hotels are cheaper but very variable in quality. It is not usually advisable to go for the cheapest available in more remote areas, and it is sensible to look at the room before registering. In popular tourist resorts you can stay at a *pansiyon* (guest house).

Exercises

1 You are at a travel agency.

YOU	*(Ask if there is a plane to Antalya.)*
TRAVEL AGENT	Evet efendim.
YOU	*(Ask at what time.)*
TRAVEL AGENT	Saat on yedide.
YOU	*(Say 'O.K.', and ask for a ticket.)*
TRAVEL AGENT	Peki efendim. Gidiş mi?
YOU	*(Say 'single' and ask how much it is.)*
TRAVEL AGENT	Kırk iki bin lira.
YOU	*(Hand the money over with the appropriate expression and say goodbye.)*

2 You are at a railway station.

YOU	*(Ask 'What time is the train to Ankara?')*
TICKET CLERK	Saat yirmi birde efendim.
YOU	*(Ask how much it is.)*
TICKET CLERK	Gidiş on bin, gidiş dönüş on sekiz bin. Gidiş mi?
YOU	*(Say 'No, return, please'.)*
TICKET CLERK	Buyurun efendim.
YOU	*(Ask where the Ankara train is.)*
TICKET CLERK	Ankara treni beşinci peronda efendim.
YOU	*(Ask how long it will take.)*
TICKET CLERK	Sekiz buçuk saat sürer.
YOU	*(Say 'Thank you'.)*
TICKET CLERK	Bir şey değil.

Now where do you go?

3   You are at a hotel.

RECEPTIONIST   Hoş geldiniz efendim, buyurun.
YOU   *(Do you have a vacant room?)*
RECEPTIONIST   Kaç kişi için?
YOU   *(For three people.)*
RECEPTIONIST   Kaç gece için?
YOU   *(For two nights and with bath, please.)*
RECEPTIONIST   Maalesef banyolu odamız yok.
YOU   *(Do you have a room without a bath?)*
RECEPTIONIST   Bir dakika. Evet, var efendim.
YOU   *(How much is it?)*
RECEPTIONIST   Kırk beş bin lira.
YOU   *(Fine, thank you.)*

4   How would you say:

(a) I want a room for twelve days.
(b) There is no vacant room.
(c) I want to go to the airport.
(d) Is the airport very far?
(e) I want to go by taxi.

Traditional-style house in Istanbul

6 Meeting people

Key words and phrases

To say 'I'm pleased to meet you'
Memnun oldum.

To ask 'How are you?'
Nasılsınız?

To say 'I'm fine, thank you'
İyiyim, teşekkür ederim.

To ask 'What's your name?'
İsminiz ne?/Adınız ne?

To say 'My name is . . .'
İsmim . . ./Adım . . .

To ask 'Where are you from?'
Nerelisiniz?

To say 'I am from Izmir'
İzmirliyim.

To ask 'What work do you do?'
Ne iş yapıyorsunuz?

Conversations

1 Two men, Ali and Erkan, meet for the first time.

ERKAN Ben Erkan. İsminiz[1] ne?
ALI Memnun oldum. İsmim[2] Ali.
ERKAN Memnun oldum. Nasılsınız[3]?
ALI İyiyim[4], teşekkür ederim. Siz nasılsınız?
ERKAN Ben de iyiyim, teşekkür ederim.

2 Would you like some tea or coffee?

ERKAN Bir kahve veya çay ister misiniz?
ALI Teşekkür ederim. Çay lütfen.

3 Where are you from?

ALI Nerelisiniz?
ERKAN İstanbulluyum[5]. Siz nerelisiniz?
ALI Ben İzmirliyim.

4 What work do you do?

ALI Ne iş yapıyorsunuz?
ERKAN Doktorum. Siz?
ALI Ben öğretmenim.

5 Are you married and do you have children?

ERKAN Evli misiniz[6]?
ALI Evet, siz?
ERKAN Hayır, evli değilim, bekârım. Çocuklarınız
var mı[7]?
ALI İki kızım var.

6 Where are you staying and for how long?

ERKAN Bodrum'da nerede kalıyorsunuz?
ALI Ege otelinde kalıyorum.
ERKAN Kaç gün kalıyorsunuz?
ALI On beş gün.

7 And arranging to meet the next day.

ALI Yarın nerede buluşuyoruz?
ERKAN Burada.
ALI Saat kaçta?
ERKAN Beş buçukta.
ALI Peki, allahaısmarladık.
ERKAN Güle güle.

8 Introducing people to each other: my friend . . ., my wife . . .

MAN Arkadaşım Mehmet. Eşim Emel.
MAN Memnun oldum. Eşim Ayşe.
MAN Memnun oldum.

9 Another introduction.

MAN   Doktor Ahmet.   Arkadaşım Hasan.
DOCTOR   Memnun oldum efendim.
MAN   Memnun oldum.   Nerelisiniz?
DOCTOR   Marmarisliyim.   Ne iş yapıyorsunuz?
MAN   Mühendisim.

Word list

arkadaş	friend
bekâr	single
ben	I (am)
buluşuyoruz	we meet
çocuk	child
değil	not
değilim	I'm not
doktor	doctor
Ege	Aegean
eş	spouse
evli	married
iş	work, job
isim/ad	name
kalıyorsunuz	you are staying
kız	girl
mühendis	engineer
nasıl	how
nereli?	where from?
öğretmen	teacher
siz	you (formal sing. or pl.)
veya	or
yapıyorsunuz	you do

Explanations

1 To say 'your . . .', add *-iniz* (or *-ınız, -unuz, -ünüz*) to the relevant noun:

ev	house	*ev**iniz***	your house
isim	name	*ism**iniz***	your name

If the noun ends in a vowel, just add *-niz, -nız*, etc:

| *oda* | room | *oda**nız*** | your room |

2 To say 'my . . .', you add -im [or -ım, -um, -üm]:

arkadaş	friend	arkadaşım	my friend
eş	spouse	eşim	my husband/wife
iş	work	işim	my job
isim	name	ismim	my name

If the noun already ends in a vowel, just add -m:

oda	room	odam	my room

3 To say 'How are you?' use nasılsınız?
The answer will be:
İyiyim, teşekkür ederim   I'm fine, thank you.
Teşekkür ederim   Thanks (for asking)
In return, you ask:
Siz nasılsınız?   How are you?

4 To say 'I am . . .', you add -im (or -ım, -um, -üm)
to the relevant adjective or noun:

bekâr	single	bekârım	I'm single
doktor	doctor	doktorum	I'm a doctor
öğretmen	teacher	öğretmenim	I'm a teacher

If the word ends in a vowel, an extra -y- is added
(to give -yim, -yım, etc):

iyi	good, well	iyiyim	I'm well

'I am not . . .'   is değilim
iyi değilim   I'm not well

5 To say which town you come from, you put -li
(or -lı, -lu, -lü) after the name of the town:

Londralı	Londoner	Londralıyım I'm a Londoner
Ankaralı	person from Ankara	Ankaralıyım I'm from Ankara

6 To say 'Are you . . ?', use . . . misiniz? (. . .
musunuz etc.):

Evli misiniz?	Are you married?
Ankaralı mısınız?	Are you from Ankara?
Türk müsünüz?	Are you Turkish?

7 The verb 'have' is conveyed by using *var* ('there is/are') and *yok* ('there isn't/aren't') with the possessives:

işim var	I've got a job
işim yok	I haven't got a job
çocuk child	çocuklar children
Çocuklarınız var mı?	Have you got any children?
Odanız var mı?	Have you got a room?

So if you want to know whether the café sells beer, you could say:

Bira var mı?	Is there any beer?

Or:

Biranız var mı?	Do you have any beer?

Worth knowing

Turks are generally rather more formal than the British. In a private house, you should stand up when an older person or (if you are a man) a woman either enters the room or hands you tea, coffee, sweets, etc. Shaking hands is as in most parts of Europe. When you are introduced, say *memnun oldum* ('happy to meet you') or *nasılsınız?* ('how are you?')

In provincial and more traditional parts of Turkey, it is normal to use the international Moslem greeting *selamünaleyküm* ('peace be with you'). The only appropriate reply is *aleykümselam* ('peace be with you too'). In such areas, a visiting man will not normally shake hands with a woman.

Like many European languages, Turkish has an informal 'you' (*sen*) and a formal 'you' (*siz*). You will probably be frequently addressed as *sen*, particularly by people older than you and in rural areas. But you should play safe yourself and, if in doubt, address people as *siz*, particularly if they are officials, or older than you. The most formal way to address someone is to use *Sayın* with their surname, *Sayın Öztürk* (Mr/Mrs/Miss Öztürk). A more relaxed but still very respectful way to address an elder or equal is to use the first name, followed by *Bey* (for a man) or *Hanım* (for a woman): *Ali Bey, Ayşe Hanım*. The formal *siz* should be used with *Bey* and *Hanım*. *Bay* (Mr) and *Bayan* (Mrs/Miss/Ms) with the surname are not widely used except for foreigners: *Bay Smith, Bayan Brown*. In rural areas, you may find yourself addressed rather more informally, but still with respect, as *ağabey* ('elder brother': often pronounced *abi*), or *abla* ('elder sister'). As you get older, this is replaced by *amca* ('uncle') or *teyze* ('aunt').

If you want to smoke in the presence of others, offer them a cigarette first. In rural and traditional areas, if you are invited into a private house, you will be expected to remove your shoes – as when entering a mosque – so as to avoid carrying dirt into the house.

Exercises

1 Answer the following questions.

(a) Nasılsınız?
(I am fine, thank you.)

(b) İsminiz ne?
(My name is . . .)

(c) Londralı mısınız?
(Yes, I am a Londoner.)

(d) Evli misiniz?
(No, I am single.)

2 Ask the questions that could produce the following answers.

(a) (. . . . .)
İzmirliyim.

(b) (. . . . .)
Öğretmenim.

(c) (. . . . .)
Hayır, evliyim.

(d) (. . . . .)
Yarın yedide buluşuyoruz.

(e) (. . . . .)
Burada.

3 What are the following times of day?

(a) at 7

(b) at 11.30

(c) at 9

(d) at 5.30

(e) at 12.30

4 What would the people from the following towns be?

(a) from Istanbul

(b) from London

(c) from Bodrum

(d) from Birmingham

(e) from Konya

(f) from Marmaris

5 Tell someone that you are . . .:

(a) a doctor

(b) a teacher

(c) an engineer

Test :
Can you get by?

Ordering your drinks

1) Call the waiter.
2) Order two teas.
3) Order a Turkish coffee with no sugar.
4) Ask if they have any beer.
5) Order three beers and two Turkish coffees: one medium, one sweet.
6) Ask if they have instant coffee.
7) Order one instant coffee with milk.
8) Order a bottle of water.
9) Ask if they have a large one.
10) Ask for the bill.
11) Hand over the money and say 'keep the change'.

Eating out

12) Say 'good morning'.
13) Say you want breakfast.
14) Ask if they have eggs.
15) Order butter, honey, toast and tea.
16) Ask for a little cold milk.

Ask for the following:
17) A lentil soup, a mixed grill.
18) Grilled fish and a bottle of cold white wine.
19) Steak and mixed salad.
20) A large bottle of red wine and two bottles of mineral water.
21) Ask if they have any fruit.
22) Say 'that is enough, thank you'.

Shopping

Ask the price of:
23) . . . that large plate
24) . . . that small coffee pot
25) . . . half a kilo of peaches

26) . . . a postcard to Britain
27) . . . this map of Istanbul

Say:
28) Hello!
29) I want a black bag.
30) Is there a cheaper one?
31) Is there a bigger one?
32) What colour is that?
33) Thank you, goodbye.

Visiting sites

34) Ask for two tickets.

Say:
35) Where is Topkapi Palace?
36) Where is the mosque?
37) Where is the mosque entrance?
38) Is the mosque open?
39) Is the museum open every day?
40) How much is the entrance fee?
41) Where is the beach?
42) Is the beach far?
43) Is there a bus to the beach?
44) Where is the bus-stop?
45) The beach is a little further on. Go straight
on, it is on the right.

Travelling

Ask for the following:
46) Two return tickets to Ankara.
47) A room for four days.
48) A room for two with bath.

Say:
49) Is there a plane to Istanbul?
50) How long does it take?
51) How can I get to the station?
52) Is it far?
53) Excuse me, what time is it?
54) I don't know.
55) I want a room for six nights.
56) What time is the bus to Efes?

Meeting people

Say:

57) My name is . . .
58) How are you?
59) I am fine, thank you.
60) Would you like some tea?
61) Where are you from?
62) I am from Istanbul.
63) Are you single?
64) No, I am married.
65) Do you have children.
66) What work do you do?
67) I am an engineer.

Topkapı Sarayından
Çiniler
(Tiles from
Topkapı Palace)

Basic Turkish grammar

Nouns and adjectives

Adjectives always come before the noun:

sıcak su	hot water
siyah çanta	the black bag

When there is more than one adjective, the most important one comes first:

soğuk beyaz şarap	cold white wine

The plural is formed by adding -ler or -lar:

otel	hotel	*oteller*	the hotels
masa	table	*masalar*	the tables

But when there is a number, the noun stays in the singular:

iki otel	two hotels
beş masa	five tables

Comparatives (-er, more)

daha iyi	better
daha güzel	more beautiful, nicer

For 'than', the ending -*den* (-*dan*, -*ten*, -*tan*) is used:

*İstanbul Londra'**dan** daha sıcak.*	İstanbul is hotter than London.
*Bu lokanta o lokanta**dan** daha ucuz.*	This restaurant is cheaper than that restaurant.

Superlatives (-est, most)

en iyi	best	*en ucuz*	cheapest

Hangi oda en ucuz?	Which room is cheapest?
Bodrum'da hangi plaj en güzel?	Which beach in Bodrum is the nicest?

Demonstratives (this/that/these/those)

bu	this/these	*bunlar*	these ones
şu ⎫ *o* ⎭	those	*şunlar* ⎫ *onlar* ⎭	those ones

Bu otel çok güzel.	This hotel is very nice.
Bu oteller çok güzel.	These hotels are very nice.
Bu şarap soğuk.	This wine is cold.
Bunlar soğuk.	These are cold.

Pronouns

ben	I
sen	you
o	he/she/it
biz	we
siz	you
onlar	they
bana	to/for me
sana	to/for you
ona	to/for him/her/it
bize	to/for us
size	to/for you
onlara	to/for them

Words like 'to', 'from', 'on', 'in', 'at', 'of', 'with', 'by' are all endings in Turkish; they are added on to the words they go with. Proper nouns take an apostrophe before the ending.

to (*-ye, -ya, -e, -a*)

eve	(to) home
plaja	to the beach
Londra'ya	to London
İstanbul'a	to Istanbul

from (*-den, -dan, -ten, -tan*)

evden	from home
plajdan	from the beach
Londra'dan	from London
İstanbul'dan	from Istanbul

in, on, at (*-de, -da, -te, -ta*). ('In', 'on', 'at' are expressed by the same ending in Turkish.)

evde	at home
plajda	on the beach
sokakta	in the street
sütte	in the milk

with, by (*-yle, -le, -yla, -la*)

trenle	by train
uçakla	by plane
arabayla	by car
otobüsle	by bus
Ali'yle	with Ali
John'la	with John

of (*-nin, -nın, -nun, -nün*)

(*-in, -ın, -un, -ün*)

evin	of the house (the house's)
adamın	the man's
Bodrum'un	of Bodrum (Bodrum's)
Ali'nin	Ali's

When two nouns come together, one qualifying the other, the second noun takes the *-si, -i* (or variations) endings:

Hilton Oteli	the Hilton Hotel
İş Bankası	the İş (work) Bank
domates çorbası	tomato soup
et lokantası	meat restaurant

Possessives

Both the possessor and the thing possessed take endings:

Ali'nin lokantası   Ali's restaurant

In English, Ali takes the ending *-'s* or the word 'of' is inserted. In Turkish, Ali, the possessor, takes the *-nin/-in* (etc.) ending, and *lokanta* takes the ending *-ı/-sı* (with its variations *-i, -u, -ü, -si, -su, -sü*):

odanın kapısı	the door of the room
otelin odaları	the rooms of the hotel

To say 'my house', 'his bag' etc, the noun has to have an ending which is different for each person:

evim	my house	odam	my room
evin	your house	odan	your room
evi	his (etc.) house	odası	his (etc.) room
evimiz	our house	odamız	our room
eviniz	your house	odanız	your room
evleri	their house	odaları	their room

To say 'I am . . .', 'you are . . .', each person has a different ending:

iyiyim	I am well	doktorum	I'm a doctor
iyisin	you are well	doktorsun	you're a doctor
iyi(dir)	he/she/it is well	doktor(dur)	he/she's a doctor
iyiyiz	we are well	doktoruz	we're doctors
iyisiniz	you are well	doktorsunuz	you're doctors
iyi(dirler)	they are well	doktor(durlar)	they're doctors

(The -dir ending meaning 'he/she/it is' is not used in colloquial speech. To say 'the sea is warm', you just say deniz sıcak. 'My friend is well' is arkadaşım iyi.)

The negative of this is formed with değil; and in that case değil takes the person endings:

iyi değilim	I am not well
iyi değilsin	you are not well
iyi değil	he/she/it is not well
iyi değiliz	we are not well
iyi değilsiniz	you are not well
iyi değiller	they are not well

Questions are formed with *mi (mı, mu, mü)*. In writing, you separate the word immediately before *mi*.

iyi misin?	are you well?
iyi mi?	is he/she/it well?
iyi misiniz?	are you well?
iyiler mi?	are they well?
Yorgun musun?	Are you tired?
Ucuz mu?	Is it cheap?
Antalya'da mıyız?	Are we in Antalya?
Bekâr mısınız?	Are you single?
Güç mü?	Is it difficult?

Var and *yok*

These words have two meanings:

1 there is/are and there isn't/aren't

Bugün balık yok, ama ızgara köfte var.	Today there isn't any fish, but there are hamburgers.

2 have/has and have not/has not: with the appropriate possessive endings (my, your, his, etc):

Evim var.	I have a house
Param yok.	I haven't any money.
Biramız yok.	We have no beer.
Çocuklarınız var mı?	Do you have children?
Boş odanız var mı?	Do you have a vacant room?
Maalesef boş odamız yok.	Unfortunately we have no vacant rooms.

With **question words** like *kaç* (how many), *nerede* (where), *nereye* (to where), *ne* (what), *kim* (who), *kimin* (whose), you don't use the *mi* question ending.

Bu çanta kaç lira?	How much is this bag?
Bu oda kimin?	Whose room is this?
Ne var?	What is there? (What do you have?)

Verbs

In a dictionary you will often find verbs with the *-mek* or *-mak* ending. This means 'to': *gelmek* 'to come', *istemek* 'to want', etc. When you want to make a sentence in, for instance, the past or present tense, you remove the *-mek, -mak* ending and add a) the tense and b) the person ending:

isti (want)   *yor* (present)   *um* (person)

N.B. the verb is *iste*, but before *-yor* it comes *isti-*.

istiyorum	I want
istiyorsun	you want
istiyor	he/she/it wants
istiyoruz	we want
istiyorsunuz	you want
istiyorlar	they want
ne istiyorsunuz?	what would you like?

Past tense

The ending for the past is *-di* (or *-dı, -du, -dü, -ti, -tı, -tu, -tü*).

istedim	I wanted
istedin	you wanted
istedi	he/she/it wanted
istedik	we wanted
istediniz	you wanted
istediler	they wanted

Negatives with verbs

You put the ending *-me* (or *-ma*) after the verb and before the tense ending (before the *-yor* ending, *-me* becomes *-mi* or *-mı, -mu, mü*):

İstemiyorum.	I don't want.
Londra'ya gitmiyorum, İstanbul'a gidiyorum.	I am not going to London, I am going to Istanbul.

Imperatives

The verb is used in its plain form without the *-mek* (or *-mak*) ending.

Git!	Go! (you singular/informal)
Gidin!	Go! (you plural or formal)

Days of the week

Pazartesi	Monday
Salı	Tuesday
Çarşamba	Wednesday
Perşembe	Thursday
Cuma	Friday
Cumartesi	Saturday
Pazar	Sunday

Months of the year

Ocak	January
Şubat	February
Mart	March
Nisan	April
Mayıs	May
Haziran	June
Temmuz	July
Ağustos	August
Eylül	September
Ekim	October
Kasım	November
Aralık	December

The seasons

ilkbahar	spring
yaz	summer
sonbahar	autumn
kış	winter

Numbers

0	*sıfır*	9	*dokuz*
1	*bir*	10	*on*
2	*iki*	11	*on bir*
3	*üç*	12	*on iki*
4	*dört*	13	*on üç*
5	*beş*	14	*on dört*
6	*altı*	15	*on beş*
7	*yedi*	16	*on altı*
8	*sekiz*	17	*on yedi*

18	on sekiz	70	yetmiş
19	on dokuz	80	seksen
20	yirmi	90	doksan
30	otuz	100	yüz
40	kırk	1000	bin
50	elli	million	milyon
60	altmış		

Any number is always followed by a singular noun:

iki çay	two teas
on beş gün	fifteen days
üç bin dört yüz elli beş lira	3455 lira
bin bir gece	a thousand and one nights

Public signs

Here are some of the words you might see on public signs and notices:

mönü	menu
yemek listesi	
lokanta	restaurant
restoran	
otel	hotel
pansiyon	boarding house
tuvalet	toilets
bay	gents
bayan	ladies
boş	vacant
dolu	engaged, occupied
meşgul	
giriş	entry
çıkış	exit
dur	stop, halt
yasak	forbidden
durmak yasaktır	stopping forbidden/no stopping
girmek yasaktır	entry forbidden/no entry
fotoğraf çekmek yasaktır	no photographs
sigara içmek yasaktır	no smoking
park etmek yasaktır	no parking
denize girmek yasaktır	no swimming
açık	open
kapalı	closed
itiniz	push
çekiniz	pull
çalışma saatleri	hours of opening (*lit.* work hours)
banka	bank
vezne	cash point
postane (abb. PTT)	post office

telefon	telephone
şehirlerarası	inter-city
milletlerarası	international
uluslararası	
telgraf	telegram
mektup	letters
pul	stamps
şehir içi	local (of letters, calls)
yurtiçi	inland
yurtdışı	abroad
danışma	information
turizm bürosu	tourist office
bilet	ticket
gişe	ticket office
istasyon	station
eczane	chemist
hastane	hospital
havaalanı	airport
karakol	police station
yaya geçidi	pedestrian crossing

Answers
to exercises and test

Chapter 1

1 (a) Garson! *Or* Garson, bakar mısınız?
    (b) Bir sade kahve lütfen.
    (c) Hesap lütfen.
    (d) Teşekkürler.

2 (a) 110
    (b) 306
    (c) 500
    (d) 901
    (e) 5500
    (f) 10 000
    (g) 4000

3 (a) Bira var mı?
        İki kahve lütfen.
        Bir orta, bir şekerli.
    (b) Bakar mısınız?
        İki çay, bir neskafe lütfen.
        Sütsüz lütfen.
    (c) Garson, bakar mısınız?
        Üç bira lütfen.
        Ne var?
        Meyve suyu var mı?
        Portakal lütfen.
    (d) Garson.
        Bir şişe su lütfen.
        Küçük lütfen.
        Türk kahvesi var mı?
        İki orta lütfen.
    (e) Garson, hesap lütfen.
        Buyurun, üstü kalsın.
        Teşekkür ederim.

Chapter 2

1 (a) Günaydın.
    (b) İyi akşamlar.
    (c) İyi günler.

2 (a) Kahvaltı istiyorum lütfen.
        Tereyağı, bal, iki yumurta, kızarmış ekmek.
        Çay ve biraz süt lütfen.

(b) Hoş bulduk. Mönü lütfen.
Karışık ızgara, patates tava, patlıcan salatası.
Şarap var mı?
Bir küçük şişe kırmızı şarap lütfen.
(c) İyi akşamlar. Izgara ne var?
Izgara köfte, patates tava, karışık salata lütfen.
O kadar.

3 (a) döner kebap (not for breakfast)
(b) portakal (not a grill)
(c) kırmızı şarap (not a starter)
(d) çay (not alcoholic)

Chapter 3

1 (a) Yarım kilo domates lütfen.
(b) Bir kilo üzüm.
(c) Dört yumurta.
(d) Üç yüz gram beyaz peynir.
(e) Hepsi ne kadar?

2 (a) Bu büyük tabak kaç lira? (or Kaça? or Ne kadar?)
(b) Siyah çanta kaç lira?
(c) Küçük cezve kaç lira?
(d) Yarım kilo elma kaç lira?
(e) Bir şişe kırmızı şarap kaç lira?

3 (a) 3650
(b) 280
(c) 1250
(d) 29 740
(e) 150 815

4 İyi günler.   Bu tabak kaç lira?
Çok güzel ama biraz pahalı.
Ne kadar?
Peki, iyi.   Buyurun.
Allahaısmarladık.

Chapter 4

1 (a) Bağdat Caddesi nerede?
(b) Cami nerede?
(c) Cami girişi nerede?
(d) Otobüs durağı nerede?
(e) Müze nerede?

2 (a) Az ileride.
(b) Sağda.
(c) Solda üçüncü cadde.
(d) Düz gidin.
(e) İki yüz metre sonra (or ileride).

3 (a) Cami açık mı?
    (b) Ne zaman açılır?
    (c) Giriş ne kadar?
    (d) Giriş nerede?

4 (a) 3 o'clock
    (b) 8 o'clock
    (c) from 9 o'clock till 1 o'clock
    (d) until 3 o'clock
    (e) three hours later/in three hours time
    (f) four days later
    (g) from 10 o'clock to 8 o'clock

5 (a) Affedersiniz. Plaja gitmek istiyorum.
    (b) Plaj nerede?
    (c) Plaja otobüs var mı?
    (d) Uzak mı?
    (e) Teşekkür ederim.

6 Affedersiniz.   Müze ne zaman açık?
   Hergün mü?
   Giriş ne kadar?
   Giriş nerede?
   Teşekkür ederim.   Allahaısmarladık.

Chapter 5

1 Antalya'ya uçak var mı?
   Saat kaçta?
   Peki, bir bilet lütfen.
   Gidiş. Ne kadar?
   Buyurun. Allahaısmarladık.

2 Ankara'ya tren saat kaçta?
   Ne kadar?
   Hayır, gidiş dönüş lütfen.
   Ankara treni nerede?
   Ne kadar sürer?
   Teşekkür ederim.
   Platform 5.

3 Boş oda var mı?
   Üç kişi için.
   İki gece için, banyolu lütfen.
   Banyosuz oda var mı?
   Ne kadar?
   Peki, teşekkür ederim.

4 (a) On iki gün için bir oda istiyorum.
    (b) Boş oda yok.
    (c) Havaalanına gitmek istiyorum.
    (d) Havaalanı çok uzak mı?
    (e) Taksiyle gitmek istiyorum.

Chapter 6

1 (a) İyiyim, teşekkür ederim.
   (b) İsmim . . .
   (c) Evet, Londralıyım.
   (d) Hayır, bekârım.

2 (a) Nerelisiniz?
   (b) Ne iş yapıyorsunuz?
   (c) Bekâr mısınız?
   (d) Yarın saat kaçta buluşuyoruz?
   (e) Nerede?

3 (a) Yedide.
   (b) On bir buçukta.
   (c) Dokuzda.
   (d) Beş buçukta.
   (e) Yarımda.

4 (a) İstanbullu.
   (b) Londralı.
   (c) Bodrumlu.
   (d) Birminghamlı.
   (e) Konyalı.
   (f) Marmarisli.

5 (a) Doktorum.
   (b) Öğretmenim.
   (c) Mühendisim.

'Can you get by?'

(1) Garson, bakar mısınız?
(2) İki çay lütfen.
(3) Bir sade Türk kahvesi.
(4) Bira var mı?
(5) Üç bira, iki kahve; bir orta, bir şekerli.
(6) Neskafe var mı?
(7) Bir sütlü neskafe.
(8) Bir şişe su.
(9) Büyük var mı?
(10) Hesap lütfen.
(11) Buyurun, üstü kalsın.
(12) Günaydın.
(13) Kahvaltı istiyorum lütfen.
(14) Yumurta var mı?
(15) Tereyağı, bal, kızarmış ekmek ve çay lütfen.
(16) Biraz soğuk süt lütfen.
(17) Mercimek çorbası, karışık ızgara.
(18) Izgara balık ve bir şişe soğuk beyaz şarap.
(19) Biftek ve karışık salata.
(20) Bir büyük şişe kırmızı şarap ve iki şişe maden suyu.

(21) Meyve var mı?
(22) Bu kadar yeter, teşekkür ederim.
(23) Şu büyük tabak ne kadar?
(24) Şu küçük cezve kaç lira?
(25) Yarım kilo şeftali ne kadar?
(26) İngiltere'ye posta kartı kaç lira?
(27) Bu İstanbul haritası kaç lira?
(28) Merhaba!
(29) Bir siyah çanta istiyorum.
(30) Daha ucuz var mı?
(31) Daha büyük var mı?
(32) Şu ne renk?
(33) Teşekkür ederim, allahaısmarladık.
(34) İki bilet lütfen.
(35) Topkapı Sarayı nerede?
(36) Cami nerede?
(37) Cami girişi nerede?
(38) Cami açık mı?
(39) Müze hergün açık mı?
(40) Giriş ne kadar?
(41) Plaj nerede?
(42) Plaj uzak mı?
(43) Plaja otobüs var mı?
(44) Otobüs durağı nerede?
(45) Plaj az ileride. Düz gidin, sağda.
(46) Ankara'ya gidiş dönüş iki bilet lütfen.
(47) Dört gün için bir oda lütfen.
(48) İki kişi için banyolu bir oda lütfen.
(49) İstanbul'a uçak var mı?
(50) Ne kadar sürer?
(51) İstasyona nasıl giderim?
(52) Uzak mı?
(53) Affedersiniz, saat kaç?
(54) Bilmiyorum.
(55) Altı gece için bir oda istiyorum.
(56) Efes'e otobüs saat kaçta?
(57) İsmim . . .
(58) Nasılsınız?
(59) İyiyim, teşekkür ederim.
(60) Çay ister misiniz?
(61) Nerelisiniz?
(62) İstanbulluyum.
(63) Bekâr mısınız?
(64) Hayır, evliyim.
(65) Çocuklarınız var mı?
(66) Ne iş yapıyorsunuz?
(67) Mühendisim.

Word lists

English–Turkish

This is far from being a complete list of the words in this book. It is a selection of the words you are most likely to look up for the exercises.

A	aeroplane	*uçak*
	airport	*havaalanı*
	apple	*elma*
	aubergine	*patlıcan*
B	bag	*çanta*
	bank	*banka*
	bath(room)	*banyo*
	beach	*plaj*
	beautiful	*güzel*
	beer	*bira*
	big	*büyük*
	bill	*hesap*
	black	*siyah*
	blue	*mavi*
	boarding house	*pansiyon*
	boat	*vapur*
	bottle	*şişe*
	bread	*ekmek*
	breakfast	*kahvaltı*
	bus	*otobüs*
	bus stop	*otobüs durağı*
	butter	*tereyağı*
C	car	*araba*
	carpet	*halı*
	cheap	*ucuz*
	cheese	*peynir*
	child	*çocuk*
	closed	*kapalı*
	coffee	*kahve*

coffee pot	*cezve*
cold	*soğuk*
colour	*renk*
cup	*fincan*
D day	*gün*
E egg	*yumurta*
entrance, entry	*giriş*
F far	*uzak*
fish	*balık*
friend	*arkadaş*
fruit	*meyve*
fruit juice	*meyve suyu*
G girl	*kız*
glass	*bardak*
grapes	*üzüm*
green	*yeşil*
grill(ed)	*ızgara*
H here	*burada*
honey	*bal*
hors d'oeuvres	*meze*
hotel	*otel*
house	*ev*
how?	*nasıl?*
how much?	*ne kadar? kaça? kaç lira?*
husband	*eş*
J jacket	*ceket*
L leather	*deri*
left	*sol*
lentil	*mercimek*
lovely	*güzel*
M map	*harita*
meat	*et*
melon	*kavun*
menu	*mönü, yemek listesi*
milk	*süt*
minute	*dakika*

	money	*para*
	mosque	*cami*
	museum	*müze*
N	name	*ad, isim*
	no	*hayır*
O	olive	*zeytin*
	open	*açık*
	orange	*portakal*
P	palace	*saray*
	passport	*pasaport*
	peach	*şeftali*
	pepper	*biber*
	person	*kişi*
	plate	*tabak*
	postcard	*posta kartı*
	potato	*patates*
R	red	*kırmızı*
	restaurant	*lokanta, restoran*
	return (ticket)	*gidiş dönüş*
	right	*sağ*
S	salad	*salata*
	sea	*deniz*
	single (ticket)	*gidiş*
	(not married)	*bekâr*
	small	*küçük*
	soup	*çorba*
	stamp	*pul*
	station	*istasyon*
	steak	*biftek*
	fillet	*bonfile*
	street	*cadde*
T	taxi	*taksi*
	tea	*çay*
	there	*orada*
	ticket	*bilet*
	today	*bugün*
	tomato	*domates*
	tomorrow	*yarın*

| town | şehir |
| train | tren |

| V | vegetable | sebze |
| | very | çok |

W	waiter	garson
	water	su
	mineral water	maden suyu
	water melon	karpuz
	what?	ne?
	when?	ne zaman?
	where?	nerede?
	white	beyaz
	wife	eş
	wine	şarap

| Y | yes | evet |

Turkish – English

A	açık	open
	ad	name
	affedersiniz	excuse me
	afiyet olsun	bon appétit
	allahaısmarladık	goodbye
	altı	six
	altmış	sixty
	ama	but
	arkadaş	friend
	az	a little

B	bak	look
	bal	honey
	balık	fish
	bana	to me, for me
	banyo	bath/bathroom
	başka bir şey?	anything else?
	bekâr	single
	ben	I
	beyaz	white
	biber	pepper
	biftek	steak

	bilet	ticket
	bin	thousand
	bin yüz	one thousand one hundred
	bir	a, one
	bir şey değil	don't mention it
	bira	beer
	biraz	a little
	bonfile	fillet steak
	boş	vacant, empty
	bu	this
	bugün	today
	bu kadar	this much
	buluş	meet, get together
	bunlar	these (ones)
	burada	here
	buraya	to here
	buyurun	yes? can I help you? here you are
	büyük	large, big
C	*cadde*	road, street
	cami	mosque
	cezve	special pot for making Turkish coffee
Ç	*çanta*	bag
	çay	tea
	çocuk	child
	çok	very, a lot
	çorba	soup
D	*da*	too, as well
	daha	more
	dakika	minute
	değil	not
	deniz	sea
	doksan	ninety
	doktor	doctor
	dolma	stuffed
	dolu	engaged, occupied
	domates	tomato
	döner kebap	doner kebab

duble	double measure for drinks
düz	straight on

E

efendim	sir, madam (*or* what did you say?)
Ege	Aegean
ekmek	bread
elli	fifty
elma	apple; apple tea
en	the most, -est
eş	spouse
Ethem Efendi Caddesi	Ethem Efendi Road
evet	yes
evli	married

F

fanta	fizzy orange drink

G

garson	waiter
gece	night
giderim	I go
gidin	go (*command*)
gidiş	one-way, single
gidiş dönüş	return
giriş	entry
gitmek	to go
gram	gram
güç	difficult
güle güle	goodbye (*lit.* go with a smile)
gün	day
günaydın	good morning
güzel	beautiful, nice

H

hangi?	which?
hariç	except
harita	map
havaalanı	airport
hayır	no
hemen	at once
hepsi	all, all of it/them
hergün	every day
hesap	bill

	hoş bulduk	*set response to* hoş geldiniz (*lit.* we find you well)
	hoş geldiniz	welcome
İ	*içersiniz*	you drink
	için	for
	iki	two
	ikinci	second
	ileride	further on
	imam bayıldı	aubergine dish cooked in olive oil (*lit.* the priest has fainted)
	incir	fig
	isim	name
	İstanbullu	person from Istanbul
	ister misiniz?	would you like?
	istiyorum	I want/would like
	iş	work, job
	iyi	well, good
	iyi akşamlar	good evening
	iyi geceler	good night
	iyi günler	good day *or* goodbye (used any time throughout the day)
	iyiyim	I am well
I	*ızgara*	grill(ed)
K	*kaç?*	how much?, how many?
	kaça?	how much?
	kadar	much
	kahvaltı	breakfast
	kahve	coffee
	kal	stay
	kapalı	closed
	karışık	mixed
	karpuz	water melon
	karşıda	opposite
	kavun	melon
	kilo	kilo
	kırk	forty

kırmızı	red
kişi	person, people
kız	girl
kızarmış ekmek	toast
kola	coke
köfte	small hamburgers
küçük	small

L

lira	lira (Turkish currency unit)
Londralı	Londoner
lütfen	please

M

maalesef	unfortunately
maden suyu	mineral water
mavi	blue
memnun oldum	I am pleased (to meet you)
mercimek	lentil
merhaba	hello
merkez	centre
metre	metre
meyve	fruit
meyve suyu	fruit juice
meze	hors d'oeuvres
model	style, model
mönü	menu
mühendis	engineer
müze	museum

N

nasıl?	how?
nasılsınız?	how are you?
ne?	what?
ne kadar?	how much?
ne zaman?	when?
ne zaman açılır?	when will it open?
neli?	with what? (what flavour?)
nerede?	where?
nereden?	from where?
nereli?	where from?
nerelisiniz?	where are you from?

nereye?	where to?
neskafe	instant coffee

O *o* — that
oda	room
o kadar	that much
olur	all right
orada	there
orta	medium, medium-sweet
otobüs	bus, coach
otobüs durağı	bus stop
otuz	thirty
öğretmen	teacher

P *paket* — packet, parcel
para	money
pasaport	passport
patates	potatoes
patlıcan	aubergine
patlıcan kızartması	fried aubergine
peki	OK
peron/platform	platform
peynir	cheese
pilaki	white beans cooked in sauce
plaj	beach
portakal	orange
posta kartı	postcard
pul	stamp

R *rakı* — aniseed-flavoured alcoholic drink
renk	colour
rica ederim	don't mention it

S *sade* — without sugar, plain
sağ	right
sağ taraftan	from the right-hand side
sağol	thanks
salata	salad
Salı	Tuesday

	saray	palace
	sebze	vegetable
	seksen	eighty
	serbest	free, no charge
	sıcak	hot
	siyah	black
	siz	you (plural or formal singular)
	soğuk	cold
	sol	left
	su	water
	süt	milk
Ş	şarap	wine
	şeftali	peach
	şehir	city, town
	şeker	sugar
	şekerli	with sugar, sweet
	şey	thing
	baska bir şey	anything else
	bir şey değil	don't mention it
	şiş kebap	lamb pieces grilled on skewers
	şişe	bottle
T	tabak	plate
	tabii	of course
	taksi	taxi
	tamam	OK
	taraf	side
	tava	fried
	tereyağı	butter
	teşekkür ederim	(I) thank you
	teşekkürler	thanks
	tren	train
	Türk	Turkish
U	ucuz	cheap
	uçak	aeroplane
	uzak	far, far away
	üç	three
	üstü kalsın	keep the change
	üzüm	grapes

V	*vapur*	boat, ferry
	var	there is, there are
	ve	and
	ver	give
	verelim	let us give (you)
	veya	or
Y	*yapıyorsunuz*	you are doing, you do
	yarım	half a . . .
	yarımda	at 12.30
	yarın	tomorrow
	yetmiş	seventy
	yirmi	twenty
	yok	there isn't/aren't
	yumurta	egg
	yürüyerek	on foot
	yüz	hundred
Z	*zeytin*	olive

Other titles in the *Get by in* . . . series

Get by in Arabic
Get by in Chinese
Get by in French
Get by in German
Get by in Greek
Get by in Italian
Get by in Japanese
Get by in Portuguese
Get by in Spanish

Shortly available

Get by in Russian
Get by in Hindi and Urdu
Get by in Serbo-Croat

BBC Books publish a wide range of language books and cassettes to suit all levels. If you would like to receive a complete catalogue of BBC language courses, please write to:

BBC Books Enquiries
Room A3116
Woodlands
80 Wood Lane
London W12 0TT

Or telephone 01-576 2587